A GOODLY FELLOWSHIP

THE MACMILLAN COMPANY
NEW YORK · BOSTON · CHICAGO · DALLAS
ATLANTA · SAN FRANCISCO

MACMILLAN AND CO., Limited
LONDON · BOMBAY · CALCUTTA · MADRAS
MELBOURNE

THE MACMILLAN COMPANY
OF CANADA, Limited
TORONTO

A Goodly Fellowship

by

MARY ELLEN CHASE

❧•❧

NEW YORK · 1939

The Macmillan Company

PRINTED IN THE UNITED STATES OF AMERICA
AMERICAN BOOK—STRATFORD PRESS, INC., NEW YORK

To

WILLIAM ALLAN NEILSON

Chief among the goodly fellowship
of those who teach

The goodly fellowship of the prophets praise Thee.

Te Deum

Rest to the souls of those fine old Pedagogues; the breed, long since extinct, of the Lilys and the Linacres: who, believing that all learning was contained in the languages which they taught, and despising every other acquirement as superficial and useless, came to their task as to a sport.

Charles Lamb: *The Old and the New Schoolmaster.*

CONTENTS

THIS book is the story of a life spent in teaching. I know it well, for it is my own. I have taught now for thirty years, beginning in a rural school on the coast of Maine, concluding, although happily not ending, in Smith College. The course of these years marks not so much promotion as a normal sort of progression, since in my experience a teacher is a teacher wherever placed, and the interest aroused and held in the college classroom essentially no different from that excited and kept in the country school. In other words, the personal resources of the teacher, always more important than the intellectual, the compensations, and the fun, are very much the same.

I write this book partly because I have been encouraged to write it by persons whom I respect, mostly because I shall have a good time doing so. The first reason I state in the desire to absolve myself from the presumption always latent, to me at least, in autobiographical narratives by those relatively unimportant; the second reason is the real one. Teaching has been, and is, the good life to me; and, if only for my own pleasure, I shall enjoy putting into words my experiences in a wide variety of educational institutions. Moreover, since the past thirty years have witnessed so many changes in American education, in both schools and colleges, in both theory and practice, it may be that such a record as this will be of interest and, perhaps, of value.

I do not, however, write as one having authority on "Education" as a profession. I know little of theories and am inclined to be suspicious of those experimentalists who are forever tampering with that most personal of possessions, the human mind, and with new ways and means for its nurture. I am a teacher and not an "educator", and what I know of my job has been acquired not through experiment but through experience, not by theory but by practice.

My book is, in a sense, a complement, perhaps a sequel, to *A Goodly Heritage* written ten years ago. The material of one chapter, that on the rural school, is much the same as in the earlier book. I include it here in different form only to make the story of my teaching complete.

Like the Lilys and the Linacres, of whom Lamb speaks in his essay, *The Old and the New Schoolmaster,* there are thousands of teachers today, whatever their subjects and wherever they may be teaching, who likewise come to their task "as to a sport". They have been and remain, not among the noble army of martyrs but among the goodly fellowship of the prophets, praising whatever Gods there be. It is among these thousands, this goodly fellowship, that I hope to find my readers. It is to them, and especially to one among them, that I address and dedicate my book.

MARY ELLEN CHASE

Smith College
April, 1939

Chapter I

MY EARLIEST TEACHERS

I

MY MOTHER was my first and always my best teacher. I make this statement, not in the sentimental vein of Mothers' Day, nor yet after the deferential manner of King Solomon in praise of the virtuous woman, but merely as a fact. My mother possessed all those natural gifts and qualities which have given rise to the term "a born teacher". Her own actual experience in the art had been brief, limited to two terms in a Maine rural school, which she taught at sixteen in the year 1882 for five dollars a week, and to one year of teaching Latin in a Maine Academy. She married at eighteen; but with three children at the age of twenty-two and with five others at more comfortable intervals in the years following, she found ample scope for her talents.

In our small Maine village of Blue Hill, situated at the head of Blue Hill Bay, between those two greater arms of the Atlantic, Penobscot Bay and Frenchman's, the schools in the eighteen-nineties were precisely what one would expect of the time and place and of the nature of village society. Blue Hill, like other coast villages once known in many a remote corner of the earth because of their seafaring, had long before the turn of the century settled into an unimportant and secluded existence. The onrush of summer residents and tourists, who were soon to afford the one means of livelihood to most coast towns, had in those days hardly begun. Among the thousand inhabitants of the village a few families still lived upon what was left of the money made in shipping; but for the most part the character of its society was that of a hundred other places similarly situated and similarly endowed. There were the usual professions represented: one doctor, one dentist, two ministers, one lawyer (who was my father) and the praeceptor of the Academy. There were the usual tradesmen and shopkeepers, and the usual fishermen, some of whom sailed to the Banks, more of whom set their trawls or dropped their lines in nearer, more quiet waters. There were the farmers, whose few tough acres were cultivated hardly a mile from the village post-office as well as through the high surrounding country-side. There were two saw-mills by the stream that ran into the harbor, mills which from the timber got out of the woods in winter turned out logs, boards, and staves for the coastwise schooner trade, clapboards and shingles for local building, and "edgings" at five cents a bunch for village cookstoves and fire-places.

Marketing was simple in those days and the exchange of money almost strictly local as the nearest bank was fourteen miles away, a two-hour journey by horse and carriage through hilly country. Those who kept hens sold eggs at ten cents a dozen to their neighbors, who in turn sold them milk at five cents a quart. What meat there was was mostly native, brought to one's door in a white-covered wagon to supplement the supply of pork, bacon, sausages, ham and hogshead cheese which awaited most families in near-by pig-pens. Boys dug clams, shelled and sold them at ten cents a quart. Fishermen either peddled their early morning catch from house to house or, in their boats at the town wharf, awaited customers who bought cod and haddock at three cents a pound. When mackerel, smelts or alewives were running, heads of families looked quickly after their own tables. Butter was made in a vast majority of homes in a blue hand-churn on the kitchen floor, and to buy a loaf of bread was not only unheard-of, but impossible. Had it been possible, indeed, it would have been considered a wanton extravagance, indulged in only by the shiftless. In my childhood to harbor a "boughten" cookie in a household marked a family as already doomed to insignificance and failure!

The schools of such a village were simply its schools. They were hewn out of respectability and governed by necessity. No one thought of them as either good or bad, and without doubt they pos-

sessed qualities of both. Within the boundaries of
Blue Hill, which extended seven miles to the north
and about the same distance east and west and
which included an inhabited island or two, there
were a dozen or more district schools supported
as was that of the village proper by local taxation. In my childhood the village school, which
possessed two rooms known as the primary and the
grammar school, or as the lower and the upper
school, managed to exist for only twenty-five weeks
during the year, since there was not sufficient
money for more instruction. From late January
until early April we had the Long Vacation.

The two teachers of the village school like those
of the district schools were local women, products
for the most part of the Normal School in the
neighboring town of Castine, sixteen miles away. I
am sure that they taught me a great deal. I can still
bound Idaho at a moment's notice, still work cube
root, still locate the Falls of Nyanza, still diagram
the first twenty lines of *Paradise Lost*. I find myself on solitary walks still declaiming "The Burial
of Moses" and "Horatius at the Bridge"; in fact,
with very little prompting I can recite the three
hundred pages of Mr. T. W. Harvey's *Fifth
Reader* since, because of municipal poverty and
my early learning to read, I stayed within its covers for eight pleasant years. I shall never forget
that "the use of the monotone is chiefly confined to
grave and solemn subjects, as in 'Man that is born

of a woman is of few days and full of trouble' ".
The counties of Maine have always stood me in
great good stead, for, repeated as they should be,
they have all the dignity and resonance of Milton's
fallen angels or of Agamemnon's hosts before the
walls of Troy.

To one who, like myself, loves useless and extraneous bits of knowledge and who still believes
the memory an important part of the human
mechanism, the village school offered many blessings, for which I shall be forever grateful. I am
grateful, too, in an age when the salutary effects
of fear are questioned, for the fears which my
teachers instilled into me—the fear of careless,
untidy work, the fear of disobedience, the awful
fear of failure and subsequent disgrace. But, so
far as I can remember, my teachers in the village
school did not make me conscious of the drama in
knowledge. At a weekly wage of seven dollars, in
return for which one taught fifty unassorted children, drama, perhaps, was not included in the
price! There was, of course, plenty of drama in
school itself: in the daily spelling-classes, in the frequent imposition of punishment, in competition for
prizes, in the weekly selection of colored picture
cards for perfect performance of one's duties. But
the drama seemingly so obvious in the incidents
of history, in Antony's speech over Caesar's dead
body and in Plato's description of the death of
Socrates, both of which selections were in our

school Reader, as well as the drama hidden in the morning Psalm, was not so evident in school. That I learned at home from the teaching of my mother.

My mother, I feel sure, did not teach us at home because she was dissatisfied with our teachers at school. Like the other mothers of the village she took the school as a matter of course. She taught us because she could not help it. She was a born teacher, and we were there and ready for the exercise of her talents.

I have often thought since the days of my mother's instruction in the kitchen, in the orchard, in the dining-room how most of what I know about teaching has come from her. In the first place, she understood, perhaps unconsciously, the first and cardinal principle of all successful teaching: that in order to interest others in anything at all, one must be oneself consumed with interest. My mother's prodigal vitality brought into life and action all people, events, and places within the covers of books. No one and nothing could remain dull and lifeless once she had touched and enlivened them with her magic. Possessed alike of a fine memory and a pleasing voice, she recited the poems in Mr. Harvey's Reader so that the singsong in which we so often droned them in school became an insult to both poet and poem.

We were always reciting something or other in our Maine kitchen. On Saturday mornings we churned to anapaests:

"The Assyrian came down like the wolf on the fold,
And his cohorts were gleaming with purple and gold"

My mother sang or recited as she rolled out brown dough for ginger snaps or cut out doughnuts with swift, rhythmical turns of her capable hand. I first learned in her pantry of

"old, forgotten, far-off things
And battles long ago."

Jerusalem, the Golden, will always smell to me, not of milk and honey, but of doughnuts bobbing about upon hot fat, and in all heavy snowfalls today God again becomes a shelter from the stormy blast as He was so defined by my mother's voice in the Maine blizzards of the nineties.

My mother's imagination cast gleams and motes of light upon the worn pages of our school Speller. From her I first learned the charm and magic of certain words, the stupidity latent in others. We learned our spelling lessons around our dining-room table, which served us as a common desk in the evening.

"Multitude," said my mother. "Now that's a big, splendid word. See how big it sounds. Get your Testaments and we'll find it. 'And seeing the multitudes', great crowds, remember, 'he went up into a mountain'. Look at the word and see all the people crowding about. Now I'll find even a better

place. Listen carefully now. 'After this I beheld and lo, a great *multitude,* which no man could number, of all nations, and kindreds, and people, and tongues, stood before the throne and before the Lamb, clothed in white robes, and palms in their hands'. That's a beautiful verse, and you should learn it. You see, in the first verse the people are all crowding around in *multitudes.* They don't quite know what they are there for, so they are just *multitudes.* But in the second, even though they are all different nations and kindreds and tongues, they all know they are there to praise God, so they are just one *multitude* in white robes with palms in their hands.

"*Meander.* That's a nice word which means just what it sounds like. The brook in the back pasture *meanders;* or poor, blind Mr. Finn *meanders* coming down the road; or you *meander* around in your minds when you don't go straight at your lessons.

"*Moreover.* Well, that's a word which you can't see a picture of and which doesn't mean much of anything. Your father sometimes uses it when he argues his cases. Anyone can spell it, and it isn't worth bothering about."

My mother's interest in our studies at school and in our reading at home knew no variableness, neither shadow of turning. In this she was the best of teachers. She possessed, *moreover,* another trait of teachers at their best: she was herself an exhibitionist in the best sense of the word, a performer, an actor. She could "sell her stuff" because she was always incorporated within it.

The good teacher consciously or unconsciously recognizes the dramatic possibilities and potentialities in his profession as the mediocre or average teacher never does. He does not count it beneath his dignity to put on a show for his students; indeed, he cannot help doing this if he would, so inextricably is he merged with what he is teaching. Thus his show is not of himself, else he becomes ridiculous and his teaching empty and useless. All good teachers know the experience of interesting themselves as well as their students, a proof of the fact that they are playing the part of someone vastly bigger than themselves, the part of Euclid, or of Shakespeare, or of Plato, or of whoever else has given them power and life. In the class-room of the poor or the mediocre teacher there are always three distinct and distinguishable elements: the teacher, the subject or material which he is endeavoring to teach, and the students. In the class-room of the good teacher there is no such division. The students are caught up with the teacher in a common ownership of that which he is at once interpreting and re-creating both for them and for himself, just as in a good play the audience becomes for two hours the actors and the playwright. To play a part may be for some teachers an unpalatable idea as well as term; but true it is that in the lack of the best qualities of the actor lies their failure.

My mother could reach toward our library shelves for the Lambs' *Tales from Shakespeare* and in the act insure the continued immortality of Shakespeare and of Charles and Mary Lamb. The Immortals, indeed, owe their life eternal to just such readers and teachers as my mother! By her voice and by her quick glances from the page to see whether or not we shared the emotions common to Shakespeare, the Lambs, and her, she could arouse hatred, inspire love, stir questions, and excite veneration. She could create for us a world so much more real than our own that the familiar objects of our bedrooms looked strange when we had climbed unreal stairs to bed to dream of Shylock or of Ophelia with her scattered flowers.

While we were still young children, my mother instituted a dramatic ceremony in the participation of which we might express with her our extreme disgust and hatred for certain characters in our favorite books. This ceremony consisted in the passage of the book in question from one to another of us so that each might strike the page which chronicled outrageous behavior or a loathsome appearance. What mighty blows we gave to Mr. Murdstone after he had wielded his cruel cane! How we rejoiced at David's savage bite! The convict, who swore to cut out, roast, and eat Pip's heart and liver in the cemetery beyond the dark, flat wilderness of the marshes, received our revengeful attention as did fat Mr. Bumble, the beadle, and Mrs. Mann, who had thrust hungry Oliver in the coal-cellar on his ninth birthday. After we had meted out such swift and just treatment, we not only felt incomparably less sorrowful for our friends, Pip, Oliver, and David, but through this very act of friendship we became more a part of them and all their doings.

My mother in the nineties had never heard of the project method of teaching. She was spared both the terminology and the talk of the "new" schools. But like all good teachers, old line or progressive, she knew that what we taught ourselves through her guidance and suggestion would remain longest in our minds. She was forever encouraging us to make up new plays and games out of our lessons at school and from our books at home. We learned fractions from cutting pies and apples, and measurements from ascertaining the square or cubic feet of our own flower-beds, woodpiles, and stone-walls. On Saturday evenings we enacted historical incidents in the kitchen with our parents, grandmother, and the "hired girl" as the guessers of our tableaus and scenes. From the stories which my father read or told to us, we played Pliny's death from the falling stones of Vesuvius, and Leonidas at the Pass of Thermopylae long before we had begun the study of ancient history in the Academy.

2

My father in his regard for discipline and his
attention to detail supplemented the teaching of
my mother. As the fear of the Lord is the beginning of wisdom, so the fear of my father was the
beginning, middle, and end of our years at school.
We literally did not dare to fail in our lessons.
The disgrace at school was as nothing compared
to the scorn and anger awaiting us at home.

I am sure that my father was quite too stern a
taskmaster, for he forfeited much of our confidence
and not a little of our affection by his unremitting
insistence upon excellence and order. He loathed
untidiness in any form, an untidy appearance, an
untidy room, an untidy mind. He despised a job
half done whatever it was; he recognized apparently no easy road to any goal; and the terror of
his contempt was always with us. And yet, although
the spirit of his law was often lost in its letter,
although his teaching, unlike that of my mother,
was designed rather for fruition in the future than
in the present, we learned from him at least one
principle which in the schools and homes of today is too seldom insisted upon: that the harder a
task, the more satisfaction in its accomplishment.

His method of teaching was endless repetition;
his goal the sure and certain possession of facts.
In the strictest privacy, which admitted not even
my sisters to my confidence, I thought of him as

M'Choakumchild or even as the terrifying Thomas
Gradgrind, and of myself as poor Sissy Jupes,
whose fancy for a flowered carpet was so cruelly
put to rout. Yet with all his relentless drilling my
father managed, doubtless through his own enthusiasm, to endow these facts with life. Like the
poets and novelists of two centuries ago he
obviously looked upon a fact as enlivened by its
original meaning, an act or a deed. He had a
passion for dates and was forever demanding them
of us.

> What was the date of King Philip's War?
> When was the Missouri Compromise?
> When was the Battle of Hastings?
> What is the date of Napoleon's birth?
> When did Shakespeare die?

He constructed on cards a game of dates, which
we played with him in the evenings after our
lessons were learned or during weeks when there
was no school, so that long before many of the
dates themselves held any significance for us,
scores of them were indelibly imprinted upon our
minds. Stern as he was, he seldom withheld just
commendation, and a word of praise from him
was long to be cherished.

Actually a poor mathematician and, as I learned
later, disliking numbers heartily, he insisted on
mental arithmetic for what seemed hours at a
stretch. The nervous strain of this exercise has

remained with me always and has perhaps resulted in a total inability to subtract when "borrowing" is necessary. Beginning with the difficult, and to me especially annoying, number nine, he would race through endless computations, adding, multiplying, dividing, subtracting, his eyes darting meanwhile around our tense and frightened circle. Once lost, of course, one was gone forever, and I was more often lost than not. A certain peculiar ache between the shoulders seemed the concomitant of this ghastly pastime. I called it then the Number Nine Ache, and the name has persisted for forty years since I always suffer the familiar malady in those irritating hours before I finally acknowledge on the first of every month that the bank is a better arithmetician than I.

My father entertained an almost ruthless belief in the dignity and necessity of manual labor by each and every member of his large family. He might have said with Carlyle: "There is a perennial nobleness, even sacredness in Work". Like most other village families with a few acres of field about the house and pasturage to be had not far away we kept horses, a cow or two, and pigs. Except for the days when he was holding court, for he was Judge of the Municipal Bench, or when he was in attendance upon sessions of the State Legislature, my father cared for his stock himself— milked his cows, groomed his horses, cleaned his stable, which was always immaculate. For him it was not enough that his daughters should be well trained in household chores. He taught us, boys and girls alike, to feed, bed down, and clean, to harness and to drive, single and team. From May to November from the age of ten until I went to college, I led or drove one cow or two to pasture. We raised our own vegetables for family use, and I was taught to weed and to cultivate. We had an apple orchard, and it was unthinkable to pay for labor when there were able-bodied children to gather in the crop.

Manual labor to my father was not only good and decent for its own sake, but, as he was given to saying, it straightened out one's thoughts, a contention which I have since proved on many occasions; indeed, the best antidote I know to a confused head or to tangled emotions is work with one's hands. To scrub a floor has alleviated many a broken heart and to wash and iron one's clothes brought order and clarity to many a perplexed and anxious mind.

My father had a passion, too, for memorizing poetry and prose and continued the process himself while he was demanding the same from us. I have never known a memory like my father's. He could repeat by heart endless consecutive lines of the *Iliad* and *Odyssey,* pages of Burke and Macaulay, and most of the Bible; and he was daily adding to his store by constant reading. A poor sleeper, he read half the night and was usually declaiming something or other when he descended the stairs for his breakfast. We used to gauge his temper by the nature of his recitation. Greek hexameters invariably denoted a calm and cooperative mind whereas Lincoln's Gettysburg Address, for no discernible reason, suggested that we make our presence as unobtrusive as possible. He liked nothing better than to hear us recite the poems which we had learned at school or which he had set for us; and although there was always correction forthcoming, we were aware that he was insisting upon perfection not so much for its own sake as for the sake of the poem which he loved.

His extraordinary memory was apparent also in his remarkable power of observation. Nothing ever escaped him, and there was no source of annoyance so irritating to him as carelessness or inattention. He was forever asking minute questions and expecting clear and accurate replies: what designs were on either side of various coins, how a cow lay down, what was the appearance of certain vegetable or flower seeds, how we could distinguish one tree from another. A walk with him was the occasion for almost painful agility in seeing and hearing. As I grew older, I realized that much of this meticulousness, in so far as it had to do with things out-of-doors, arose from his love and understanding of nature. His imagination was more exhaustive than my mother's, less synthetic

than hers; yet because of him no common roadside
can ever be dull to me, no country walk unexciting.
There is a line in Katherine Mansfield's *Journals*
which speaks of the "Life in the life" of things.
This my father knew, and this, stern, reserved, and
taciturn as he was, he somehow communicated to
his children.

Once when I was ten years old and had gone to
bed in fear of the disclosure of some misbehavior,
my father woke me at midnight and ordered me
out-of-doors. I can never forget my paralysis of
fright. But when I had stumbled down the stairs
and into the field behind the house, I found the
family gathered.

It was in August, one of those nights of sudden
frost to which the Maine coast is accustomed in
late summer; and the Northern Lights were
streaming from the horizon to fill the sky with
sudden shafts of flame. Not a word was spoken as
we stood there in the cold grass of the field. My
father for once neither commanded nor explained.
My mother, I remember, wrapped a fold of her
long dressing-gown around my shoulders as we
stared together at the brilliant, moving sky.

After ten minutes of complete silence my father
led his family back to bed. His one comment then
was brief.

"Don't forget it," he said.

3

I had other teachers in my childhood of whom I have already written in *A Goodly Heritage*. It would be repetition to present them here. But I should like to tell of certain elderly women whom I knew as a child and who were set apart from the other women of the village because of a past peculiar to themselves. These were the women, common in the last century to seafaring villages and towns, who had spent much of their lives at sea with their husbands.

Even as a child I knew they were different from anyone of any age whom I had ever known, and their gifts to me deserve recognition and tribute. Not only did they add light and color to the maps in our school geographies, but above all else they suggested to me certain attitudes of mind, certain ways of thought and behavior, completely at variance with those current among village society as a whole and clearly not attributable merely to age.

My grandmother had herself spent ten years at sea, years familiar to us through her frequent stories. It was largely through her that I came to know these other women similarly endowed and to gather certain conclusions about them, conclusions which, though vague and unformed, were yet a source of relief and pleasure to my childish mind.

The qualities of my grandmother alone might

not have so impressed themselves upon me save in retrospect as I grew older. She was, after all, one of the family and hence taken for granted. But my grandmother at home and my grandmother talking and knitting with her contemporaries were two entirely different persons.

When in my early teens I drove her out to make her weekly calls and visits, I entered a new world, not a village world of paltry talk, but a world of far-flung boundaries, a world of reminiscence, of wider thinking, of a kind of humorous tranquillity, in which village opinion, even village respectability, held small importance. My grandmother and her friends were daring to a degree unknown to the women of my mother's generation or to those of their own who had spent their circumscribed lives at home. They were not hemmed in by village trifles or shocked by village misdemeanors. That hunger and thirst after righteousness, so grafted upon the New England mind by two centuries and more of precept and surviving today even among the emancipated in all manner of odd tenacities, seemed somehow not to have "taken" with them. They were to me alive and free, patient and wise, unflurried and fearless. They exchanged stories of doings in some far-off port or another, the point of which was often lost on me; but I loved the gales of laughter in which they shamelessly indulged. The narrator always poked her nearest auditor with her knitting-needle, a lovely gesture, which, I understood, denoted not only a claim upon attention but a kind of bond as well. They were a group set apart by a past common to them all, a larger past, upon the fringes of which I sat enthralled and honored. My grandmother used to warn me upon our approach toward home that I would best not repeat certain things which one or another of them had said; and I jealously guarded their confidence, feeling meanwhile a delightful sense of conspiracy.

I never forgot those afternoons in the sitting-rooms of houses built by men who had sailed the Seven Seas. Some of the few remaining sea-captains I knew also, and they, too, seemed not to belong to our tidy, enclosed life. But it was their wives or widows whom I loved and admired more. To men who earned their livelihood from the sea, its life became a matter of course; to women it meant a breaking of bonds, a sudden entrance into freedom.

These women whom I knew as a child had been too often beset by Fear itself to worry over mere fears. Dependent wholly upon wind and weather, they had waited for so long that they had forgotten how to fret. Bewildered by strange faiths in strange countries, they had long ago ceased to look upon the New England Congregational Church as the one way to God. They had played too many games with Death to cherish sure and certain notions as to the best means of dealing with life.

As I grew older and dreamed of writing books, I decided that sometime I would write of them and of their finer, larger ways of life and thought. This I have tried to do in *Mary Peters* and *Silas Crockett* in grateful acknowledgment of what they taught me long ago in their homes that faced the sea.

4

When at thirteen I entered the Academy in Blue Hill, I became at once associated with some splendid teachers. Blue Hill Academy, founded at the beginning of the last century, included itself with pride among the early and excellent academies of New England. Unlike the village school it was not entirely dependent for support upon local taxation since it possessed a reasonably decent endowment. Its teachers were carefully chosen, and without exception they were during my four years the most excellent of instructors. Needless to say, they had all been classically trained both at school and at college, regardless of the subjects which they taught us. For that matter, except for history and English and a most elementary course in chemistry, Latin, Greek and mathematics made up the bill of fare and the order of the day.

All the hundred boys and girls in the Academy of my time studied mathematics for three years. No possible exception was ever made. The few who did not study Latin, and they were very few,

were denied the privilege only on the tacit ground
of mental incapability. The great majority of us
entered upon our Latin the first year and many
of us upon our Greek the next as a matter of
course.

The "educators" of today who rule the training
of teachers in our public school systems, together
with the adherents of the so-called "progressive"
schools, whether public or private, are for the most
part sceptical of the drill-master as teacher whatever his subject. Both tend, moreover, to disparage
Classics, ostensibly on the ground that they are not
sufficiently related to modern life and living, actually, I believe, because a mastery of Latin and
Greek demands that teaching by rote and rule
which they consider unprofitable for both teacher
and student. Today learning of any sort must seemingly be made not only palatable but enticing.

In well-ordered New England families of forty
years ago children were rarely enticed by their
parents toward the performance of anything. They
did what they were told or supposed to do, and the
only enticement apparent lay in the attitude and
behavior of those who had them in charge. My
mother knew and loved Latin, and to emulate her
knowledge and enthusiasm was enticement enough
for me. My father read and recited Greek for
pleasure, and before I was ten, I was waiting for
the day when I could begin its study.

The very fact that Latin and Greek were hard

was to the well-brought-up children of my generation an added spur, enticement if you will. Forty years ago there was a more basic respect for work of all kinds than there is at present, and that respect in the minds of decent people was immeasurably deepened and strengthened if the work presented unusual difficulties. Today easy roads and short cuts to all manner of physical and mental accomplishments have tended to diminish that ardor for hard work with which parents and teachers were wont to instill their children and students.

There was, and is, surely no easy road or short cut to the mastery of Latin subjunctives and Greek irregular verbs just as there is no royal road to geometry; but since we expected none, we were not disturbed when none was forthcoming. Our teachers in the Academy were drill-masters in every sense of the word, but their unrelenting drilling did not, indeed could not, put out their light as teachers. Behind their insistence upon perfection lay a zeal and a pride in their teaching. Before both them and us stood doors ready to be opened when once we had mastered the syntax, the only available key.

It is without doubt true that much of the decline in the study of Classics can be directly traced to poor and uninspired teaching. Few studies in the preparatory and high schools are ever given such a drubbing by college freshmen as is their Latin.

From their tales of persecution and pedantry one might conclude that there are still Cornelia Blimbers and Mr. Feeders extant! I can only say that they have been less fortunate than I.

I shall never forget or cease to be grateful to my Latin teacher. Nor will scores of men and women in Blue Hill today, far from Cicero and Virgil as they may be in their work and thought. Upon her death ten years ago the freshness of her memory after thirty years brought widespread regret and sadness there as in all other places where she had taught. She came to us upon her graduation from Brown University where she had studied with Anne Crosby Emery, a Maine woman like herself, and one of the finest classical scholars and teachers in the country. She thus brought with her fire to add to her own flame.

Few students at any time or in any place have had such a grounding in Latin grammar as she gave to us; yet she set at naught the stupid notion that drill and dullness are necessarily synonymous. Once we had learned the first declensions and conjugations beyond the possibility of an error, we began writing letters and stories in Latin. We wrote diaries of certain periods in Roman history which she was teaching us at the same time during another hour. We constructed the Seven Hills from papier-mâché, the Forum and the Colosseum. We made from cardboard a Roman house with *atrium* and *peristyle* complete, with tables, couches, and lamps. We enacted Roman weddings and wrote epitaphs for the tombstones of imaginary Roman relatives and friends. And when she left us, sorrowing, to go elsewhere into wider fields than those afforded by our little village, we gave her a surprise party as proof of our affection and gratitude.

What a party that was! It is still the subject of delighted reminiscence among middle-aged men and women in Blue Hill today, who have long since forgotten all the Latin they ever knew. We gave, in fact, a Roman dinner in her honor with bills-of-fare in Latin and with Roman dishes prepared by our co-operative mothers. We made togas from sheets for all our guests and became specialists on Roman hair-dressing and Roman bearing. We reclined on couches to eat while servants properly attired from family linen closets served us. The best among us wrote votive poems, *Ave atque Vale,* for her whom we adored, to be read between the courses.

Such a party today would be termed a "project" in the terminology of the progressives and considered something unusual and new. It was neither new nor old. It was simply the natural result of good teaching by a young woman with charm, imagination, friendliness and common sense, to whom Latin was not dead or sleeping, but alive and awake, and the best possible source for projects of every sort, as properly taught it is today.

The praeceptor of the Academy was my teacher of Greek, supplemented and complemented by my father at home. The methods of both were sound and unyielding; but since they possessed a common passion for their subject and communicated that passion to me, I wanted for nothing. My father, true to his nature, never talked to me of the beauty of the language while he pounded verbs into my head. But he did not need to do so since I had heard him recite the *Iliad* as he came down the stairs. Nor as I remember him did the praeceptor have much to say to us about the lines of Homer which we read with him during my last year in the Academy. He did not tell us directly of the vitality and simplicity, the directness, symmetry, and naturalness which set Greek poetry for those who know it in a place apart. But like my father and all other good teachers he did not need to do so.

The one thing which remains most clearly in my memory of him is his translating on a snowy afternoon those familiar lines which record Hector's farewell to Andromache before his battle with Achilles:

Dear one, I pray thee be not over-sorrowful. No man against my fate shall send me to my death; but Destiny, I think, no man hath escaped.

It is probable even that I should have remembered neither the translation nor the incident had it not been that when he closed his book and sent us homeward, we saw that he had tears in his eyes.

The memory of such teachers never fades nor does gratitude toward them ever lessen. When, thirty years after their patient and bountiful ministrations, I stood among the purple flowers of Catullus' home at Sirmione, I felt the presence of Florence Rafter as well as that of the poet. Both were assuredly *homines venustiores* to me. And as I picked anemones blowing among the stones of the ancient theatre at Epidaurus, I thought of John Brackett and of how because of him I should forevermore live in a land of plenty.

Chapter II

MY FIRST EXPERIENCE IN TEACHING

II

ALL my father's ideas were fixed and sturdy. One
of them was that each of his daughters should teach
a country school either before going to college or
as an interruption between the second and third
year there. He contended, with truth as I afterwards realized, that teaching not only was the
best discipline for the retention and enlargement
of one's own meagre knowledge, but that it engendered maturity through the responsibility
which it placed squarely upon one's own shoulders. If you had anything in you at all, said my
father, three terms in a country school would bring
it out. If you had nothing, then the entrance to
college or the continuation therein was obviously
a waste both of time and of money.

Unlike my older sister, who taught her school
before she entered college, I taught mine in the
spring of my sophomore year and in the year following. I had entered the University of Maine at
seventeen to continue happily in Greek and Latin
and most unhappily in higher algebra and trigo-

nometry. I think, in fact, that my disgraceful record in college mathematics, together with a somewhat chimerical love affair, decided my father that I needed to get down to what he termed the brass tacks of life as soon as possible. He, therefore, scouted about the country in search of the most difficult rural school he could find which was in need of a teacher for the spring term. Such a school he unearthed in the village of South Brooksville, Maine, then familiarly known as Buck's Harbor, and summarily informed me that the school officials of that place had graciously, if perhaps unwisely, consented to give me a try and for my services would pay me ten dollars a week.

Buck's Harbor was a coast village, little more than a hamlet, some twelve miles from Blue Hill and situated beyond Eggemoggin Reach in the neighborhood of Penobscot Bay. It has now become known as a pleasant and quiet summer resort, but in the spring of 1906, in spite of two small boarding houses, it was a native community of fishermen, small tradespeople, farmers and sailors. Most of the twenty-odd families were large and interlaced by marriage, as were most coast families in small settlements thirty years ago. The nearest academy or high school was our own, and few Buck's Harbor children in those days went beyond the rural school. There was one general store, which sheltered the post-office, and one small church, Methodist, I think, by nature, with no settled pastor. There are a hundred counterparts of just such a village on a hundred small harbors along the Maine coast.

The people of such a village were the products of their environment. In 1906 most of them were practically untouched by any outside influences since, after the manner of the Maine coast native, they looked upon their few summer visitors only with curiosity and a faint suspicion. The only persons who had been far afield, or perhaps better far afloat, were the men and boys who were deckhands on small steamers or who were engaged in fishing or in the coastwise schooner trade; and they were mostly around their own air-tight stoves in the winter. Blue Hill was to Buck's Harbor what Boston was in pre-motor days to the people of Bangor. Roads were bad in early spring and in winter often impassable. An automobile was almost as rare as an earthquake and an object of monstrous fear to the possessors of horses. Whatever distant travelling was done, and it was extremely rare, was accomplished by coastwise steamers, which in those days during the summer months brought and carried freight and passengers to a hundred village wharves now rotting and dismantled.

The school-teacher of such a village was the object of interest, terse comment, and not infrequently, at least at the start, of suspicion, particu-

larly if she had come from "away." Her appearance, manners, morals, friendliness or lack of it,
were far more important elements in her success
or failure than was any mental equipment which
she might or might not possess. Maine coast na-
tives, then even more than now, have a tendency
to assume the worst until they have become convinced that their assumption is wrong; and to
the people of Buck's Harbor a girl from college
had just that much more to live down than she
might have had as a product of the Castine Normal School or of no discernible school at all.

It was on a cold, bleak, foggy Monday morning in April, 1906, that my father deposited me,
bag and baggage, on the steps of the Buck's Harbor school-house and left me to sink or swim, sur-
vive or perish. I have often wondered since,
whether, as he drove away, the milk of human
pity had any place within his stern frame. If
there, it was not in any way apparent. His good-
bye was brief, although he did present me with
a parting gift with injunctions to use it if necessary. This gift proved to be a stout razor strop;
and without its moral as well as physical support
I should have given up teaching for good and all
one half hour after I had begun it.

My first morning in my first school was dedicated both to the theory and the practice of the
survival of the fittest. The spring was a late one,
and certain boys of sixteen or older, who other-

wise might have been at sea, were at school for a season, ostensibly to learn, actually to discover of what stuff the new teacher was made. Had my father himself been constructed of less inflexible stuff, could I have been sure of receiving understanding and sympathy at home instead of disappointment and contempt, I should then and there have run for cover, leaving the Buck's Harbor school to whatever fate awaited it.

But the fear of returning home in defeat was far more terrible than the fear of staying where I was; and I began my teaching experience with an unseemly display of passions which I had never known I possessed—anger and disgust, scorn and fury. I was a veritable Maenad in frenzy as I stormed up and down my narrow aisles. This pathetic pretense of courage, aided by the mad flourishing of the razor strop, brought forth to my amazement as though by magic the expression of respectful fear upon the faces of young giants who could have accomplished my terrified exit either by physical strength or by a like display of temper, and who had come to school with the express purpose of doing so. But no one moved to further insurrection, and although, when the reign of terror to which both forces had contributed had subsided, my quaking knees could hardly support me at my desk, I had no more trouble from discipline through eleven long weeks.

I have since wondered how a teacher, trained

in modern and more pacific ways of governing a school, would have made herself mistress of such a situation, one, moreover, whose parents possessed hearts and doors more readily open than did mine. Perhaps it is as well for the principles and the practice of the new education that district schools are fast disappearing from the American landscape. Perhaps the race is growing gentler! Surely even in the smallest of communities today there are other interests than the advent of a new teacher.

A young teacher told me recently that for other than patriotic reasons she should always look upon the American flag with respect and veneration. She said that in her first year of teaching when all other sources of interest failed and she felt herself becoming engulfed in the imminent dangers of inattention and recalcitrance, she was given to calling suddenly for a salute to the flag. She depended, she said, upon this break in affairs either to quell rising mutiny or at least to relegate it to a fresh and more easily handled start. We had no American flag at Buck's Harbor, and the now common words of salute had not yet reached our confines even if, at that date, they had been composed. But, instead of the flag, I shall always look with respect and veneration upon a razor strop, seeing in this ugly object not only the symbol of my emancipation from terror and disgrace, but as well the initial inspiration and vision which resulted two years later in my choice of a profession.

2

The school at Buck's Harbor demanded of me more mental and physical agility than mere knowledge. I had forty-nine children of all ages from five to sixteen. When I had once sorted them out in accordance with age and progress, I found myself with twenty-nine classes a day to teach. The hours from nine until four, with fifteen minutes each morning and afternoon for recess, contained all told in minutes but three hundred and thirty. This resulted even by my poor arithmetic in a maximum of eleven minutes for each class, or to be more accurate, in ten, since the classes must move in order from their seats to the bench before my desk.

Since some combination of classes must be made if any child was to learn anything at all, I conceived the notion of hearing five reading lessons in quick succession while those who were not reading were doing problems in arithmetic at the blackboards. Although the corporeal frame is subject to the boundaries of space, I soon learned that the mind can be in two or even three places at one time. One portion of my mind was riveted on the behavior of the children presumably at study in their seats; another portion fearfully scanned

the blackboards in the hope that no assistance
would be summoned; a third listened to and cor-
rected the reading of those on the bench before
me. By this method arithmetic and reading were
out of the way by the ten-thirty recess, leaving decent room for four classes in geography from ten-
forty-five until noon. I ruthlessly combined the
afternoon grammar classes, since all alike needed
the same fundamentals, and by two o'clock we had
a clear straightaway for history, which we all
liked best, and for spelling which closed the day
for everyone but me.

Needless to say, we had no frills and extras in
our school. We even had no music since the good
day of outside music teachers, even for the rural
schools, had not yet come, and since I myself could
not carry a tune. Had I been able to do so, however, we had no song or hymn books and no time.
Even the Lord's Prayer and the Bible reading
had to be hurried, so impending were arithmetic
and reading. When we were once organized, we
clicked on like a well-regulated machine from nine
until four.

I am sure that such an iron-clad program was
bad for my children; no school at any time should
be systematized to that extent. But I am equally
sure that it was the best thing that could have happened to me. I had always been a dreamy child,
given to states of absent-mindedness and particularly irritated by attention to detail. I had seem-

ingly been born with no sense of time, and the rigorous order and discipline of home and school, although I had perforce submitted to it, had not wrought the transformation hoped for by my parents. Two years of relative freedom at college had afforded blissful opportunities for the indulgence of all my worst mental habits; and the school at Buck's Harbor could not have presented itself at a more opportune moment. There was now no time for dreams of either the past or the future. It was dangerous to lose one's head for the fraction of a second. On and on the minutes raced with questions to be quickly put or as quickly answered. There was no time even for self-pity, let alone self-indulgence. For eleven weeks the stark necessity of the Buck's Harbor school held me in a never-loosened vise. When they were over, I was a different person.

3

The school-house was on a high ledge above the harbor. From its door one got a wide and lovely sweep of sea and islands, but I do not remember ever having much time to look at it. I stayed at my desk until supper time in the superintendence of dunces and in the correction of papers; and when I had once locked the school-house door, I had no extra life within me to be uplifted even by Penobscot Bay.

I boarded for two dollars and a half a week with a certain Mrs. Billings in her house below the school-house hill. She was a silent young woman with a poor complexion and with two talents which were never buried in the earth. She knit number-less baby blankets for a Portland firm, and she cooked as few women I have ever known have cooked.

For two dollars and fifty cents a week Mrs. Bill-ings stuffed me with fat, starch and sugar. She served my bountiful meals in her dining-room, but, although I assumed she ate her own in the kitchen, I never saw her eat a morsel during my residence with her, nor in her kitchen was there any sign whatever of the means of food consumption. Mrs. Billings made no distinction in her offerings for breakfast, dinner, or supper. The pork chops, fried potatoes, hot bread, doughnuts, cake, apple pie, and cheese which I had for breakfast were re-peated at noon and night with an occasional change in kind but never in bulk. School must have been more exhausting than I realized, for I was always hungry and devoured more calories than ever since in my life. I have worried for many years over Mrs. Billings' obvious lack of monetary profit by our arrangement, and have often felt that, if she still cooks in her immaculate kitchen and still knits baby blankets on her front piazza, I ought even now to set things right with her.

She housed me in her front chamber, a curiously depressing room with a huge bedstead and a feather bed and with Biblical scenes in colors, ingeniously framed in shells. I used to add to its depression through weeping at night over bank discount and compound proportion by my rickety stand with its kerosene lamp. Necessity proved, however, not so much the mother of invention in our sense of the word as the means to accomplishment; and before a month had passed I came to be, within limits and for the time being, a fairly apt arithmetician.

As the spring advanced and the roads improved, my father generously allowed me to keep our pony and cart in Mrs. Billings' barn so that I might drive home on Saturday and back again on Sunday. Perhaps he accorded me this favor because he was pleased with me, although if he was, he never divulged the fact. The pony was miraculously fed also on my two dollars and a half and by a mythical Mr. Billings, whom in eleven weeks I never saw or heard, although, since his existence was vouched for by my pupils, I presume he was extant somewhere.

Mrs. Billings and I never became friendly as she was not a talkative woman. She provided and I consumed. And, although I knew and liked the few parents of my forty-nine, I saw little of them. They were quite too busy feeding and clothing their children and getting them to school on time to pay much attention to their teacher. I think they liked me more because I made no objection to housing their pre-school youngsters than for any other reason. On most days in my school there were half a dozen babies of varying ages between two and four. The smallest of these I used to confine in large low barrels or tubs with which the village cooper provided me and from which the babies used to stare in delighted wonder at our furious educational progress.

I grew to love my charges, and I think they liked me. School to most of them was a necessary evil, alleviated only by recess and by the stories I told or read to them for two hours on Friday afternoons as a reward for good behavior. Few of them saw in it any present pleasure or any step toward the future. Like all country children they were fond of animals and flowers, and like all coast children they were shrewd in the ways of wind and weather. They could manage boats under any circumstances, though again, like most coast children, few of them could swim. Swimming, indeed, seemed but an indulgence, a pastime enjoyed by summer visitors, before whom they were always shy and sometimes rude.

I am sure I taught them very little. It was I who was educated in Buck's Harbor. But I like to remember how their sharp faces glowed on Friday afternoons over *Treasure Island* and even over *The Story of a Short Life* and *The Little Lame Prince.* Their homes were relatively bookless, and such stories as these were new fields to them. Occasionally I see certain of them now, here and there as lesser officers on summer yachts or at the county fair as stout mothers with broods of far more sophisticated sons and daughters. Three of them are teachers who, I trust, have never emulated my desperate and stumbling efforts either at discipline or at instruction.

I think I must from the beginning have looked upon teaching as a sport rather than as a respectable way of earning one's living. For on the late June Saturday when I had gathered my belongings, locked my school-house door, and harnessed my pony to drive homeward, I completely forgot to collect my wages from the First Selectman of Buck's Harbor and drove home empty-handed. My father saw in this inexcusable neglect, this disregard of one hundred and ten dollars, a proof that absent-mindedness was still with me. He sent me back that very afternoon, feeling most incompetent, to procure it. But he was somewhat less scornful when I told him upon my return that with his permission and approval I had decided to teach three more terms of school before I went back to college.

4

I taught the following year in another of the Brooksvilles, West Brooksville, just opposite Castine on the Bagaduce, a pleasant tidal river. West Brooksville was in all respects a superior village to Buck's Harbor. Like Blue Hill it had been of some importance in foreign seafaring, and in its fine old houses and in the remnants of its seafaring families it offered far more than Buck's Harbor from a social and cultural point of view.

Its schools had profited from the nature of its people. There were two of these, housed in one white building on a ledgy hill with fir woods at the back and with fields on either side. For eleven dollars a week I taught the lower school, which comprised some fifty children from five to eleven. What would now be termed the seventh and eighth grades were housed and taught in the room upstairs.

My teaching in West Brooksville was vastly easier and more pleasant, not only because my children were somewhat more of an educational unit, but also because they were mostly from families ambitious for them and of far wider experience. To most of them school was not only in itself a pleasant experience but a stepping-stone to the Academy at Blue Hill or to the high school at Castine.

I have rarely known finer children or finer people in general than those in West Brooksville. In my school here no razor strop was needed. We began by having the best possible time in school, and we continued having it throughout the year.

Only one untoward accident marred our days, and that with its concomitants became a bond among us and a source of somewhat grisly humor.

The village had been visited in September by a widespread epidemic of whooping-cough which had left no home untouched; but since all children everywhere were stricken, the school board saw no good reason, as the worst seemed over, for not opening school in early October. As all country mothers know, the "worst" of country whooping-cough contracted in September realizes no *terminus ad quem* until the spring. It continues merrily on so long as cold weather allows it no let-up.

The winter that year came early; the cold was early, too, and bitter. By late November I was breaking the ice in my pitcher to wash in the morning and hurrying in the teeth of a piercing wind to lay and to light the fire in my air-tight stove against that moment when my entire school should come whooping in. Although I had had whooping-cough as a child, I caught it again from germs or sympathy; and from November until late February we punctuated our teaching and reciting with monstrous reverberations, not to say with the frequent and loathsome accessories of whooping-cough at its height. A rural school was nothing if not prodigal in its offerings!

My year in West Brooksville also poured gifts into my lap from associations outside my schoolroom. During the autumn term I boarded with a

Mrs. Blodgett, who, although her married name is still well and favorably known in the vicinity, was herself connected with the Tapley family. Tapley is a name familiar to the coast of Maine as one of respect and honor in its maritime history. Throughout the shipping years of the last century, ship-masters and first officers of that name were well known in foreign ports all over the world as the best of men. A goodly portion of my school bore the name of Tapley, and the best of those who did not bear it retained it somewhere out of sight. The Tapleys were, in other words, the mainstay of West Brooksville and Mrs. Blodgett one of the noblest of them.

She lived a mile and more below the schoolhouse in a white story-and-a-half house on a back road. She was a tall and large woman with iron-gray hair and dark brown eyes which were a trifle out of focus. This gave her a shrewd, humorous expression, and perhaps added to her shrewdness and her humor, for she had both in large measure. She was an excellent cook, and, although she knew as little about a balanced diet as Mrs. Billings, she was not so fascinated by mere bulk.

She lived alone, her husband having died years before. She loved living alone with a passion. For that reason she had been extremely sceptical of my intrusion; but we got along famously from the start. I always connect Mrs. Blodgett in my memory and imagination with large red apples and with Charles Dickens, for the sight of either of them now inevitably recalls our many evenings together.

Mrs. Blodgett always maintained that apples were the cure for all manner of human ills, including a bad temper, and she was the proof of her contention, for she was always in the best of health and humor. She ate apples throughout the evening, crunching them loudly and with great relish, and, as she ate, she read Dickens, whom she balanced on her knees below her knitting. Dickens gave her physical as well as mental exercise. He amused and delighted her so that her ample shoulders and capacious front heaved and pitched about with her mirth which she kindly, though ineffectively, strove to control in fear of disturbing me, who was getting my lessons on the opposite side of her sitting-room table. When she could contain her enthusiasm no longer, she read me bits of whatever novel she happened to be re-reading, and we both agreed, over another apple apiece, that no one had ever lived or written like him.

She used to have my lunch ready at eight every morning in a small red pail with a distinct and charming personality of its own which I have never seen since or elsewhere in any number of pails. She gave me a very hefty sandwich containing pork or home-cured ham, two hard-boiled eggs, several cookies, hermits, or crumpets, a generous wedge of cake and always a molasses doughnut, for she considered the ordinary white doughnut harmful to the digestion. She said good-bye to me at her side-door as though she would be glad to see me back again; and as I took the short cut between the flaming sumach and maples of her pasture, I always felt grateful that I had her to come back to.

Since the winter was one of heavy snowfalls, which well-nigh obliterated both the pasture and the back road, Mrs. Blodgett in December bespoke for me the charity of Mrs. Robert Tapley, whose spacious house was near my school. Mrs. Tapley was the widow of a sea-captain, well known on the Maine coast and elsewhere as a gentleman as well as a ship-master. She herself years before had sailed with him to the Far East, and, remembering my grandmother's voyaging friends at home, I felt particularly fortunate when Mrs. Tapley consented to take me in. Mrs. Blodgett, I knew, could, like Hazlitt, never be less alone than when alone, and I left her with no anxiety over her hibernation, if with deep regret.

Mrs. Tapley was a beautiful old woman in her late seventies. She read her Bible for hours on end, I think for aesthetic rather than for ethical satisfaction and stimulus. She had lived and thought for so many years, she had seen so much of the world and its odd ways, that mere righteousness must have seemed to her not only a small word but at her age relatively a small matter. At all events through the generosity of circumstances she had gained so much of it that she did not need to give it another thought. Like my elderly friends in Blue Hill she seemed to live in a larger, calmer sphere somewhere beyond or above the trivialities of everyday existence; and when I said good night to her after a quiet evening over my lessons in the common sitting-room, I felt more than once like echoing the words of St. Peter on the Mount of the Transfiguration.

Her middle-aged daughter Harriet lived with her. She was a woman of tremendous vitality and great humor. I have rarely enjoyed anyone more. She assisted in the village post-office, played the organ in the Congregational church, instilled life and fun into the Sunday-school, cared for the family horse, cow and hens, did all the housework, shovelled snow in winter, kept a garden in summer, and found plenty of time to nurse anyone who was ill and to read prodigiously for hours on end. She was a deeply religious person without an ounce of unctuous piety, a doer of the Word but, like her mother, a hearer as well. She was fond of driving and we used to go junketing about in a smelly old sleigh to call on sick neighbors or just, as she said, "to get so we could think straighter." Like her mother she laughed away trifles and, as a result, was the first as well as the last resort in times of village trouble or tragedy.

All in all, I could hardly have spent a more

abundant year than the year in West Brooksville. When in the autumn of 1907 I returned to college, I had not only learned what I wanted from it, but was vastly better able to get what I wanted. I had lived so long by a clock that I should never again be entirely impervious to time. From a necessary obedience to rules imposed upon my existence I had learned to impose certain ones upon it myself. Through the training in holding my mind steadily to a given task, I had learned how to study. I had discovered, too, that I loved to study for the mere fun of it. Dreams and fancies, tyrannous as they were still to be, could now at least be held at bay when necessary. I could read and know what I was reading; I had begun to learn to think for myself. My sense of humor was awakened; my new sense of values was my own, cherished because I had gained it not by precept upon precept, but through the wealth as well as the rigor of a new and unique experience.

The rural school has gone never to return, at least in its original state. It has become an outworn institution, to be regarded by those who knew it more with sentiment than with respect. Where it now exists, it is no longer as it was. Its common water-pail and tin dipper have given place to more sanitary methods of assuaging country thirst. Its vitamin-less dinner-boxes have succumbed to hot lunches or at least have been supplemented by mid-morning milk. Its classes now are grades, and school buses remove to larger centers all those who are ready for the Junior High School.

Yet I am one who looks upon it, not with sentiment but with respect, respect not for the way in which it educated its children, but for the stern and agile training which it gave to its teachers. Buck's Harbor and West Brooksville did more for me than college and the graduate school combined; and I shall evermore thank them for their tolerance and my father for his unyielding common sense.

Chapter III

I SEEK MY FORTUNE IN THE MIDDLE WEST

III

WHEN I finished college in 1909, I was more
fortunate in just two respects than girls who are
now finishing college and who want to teach:
First, I had escaped those courses in the history,
science, and art of "Education" which State Boards
inflict today upon the colleges; and, second, I was
reasonably sure of a job. In all other ways, the
college graduates of this generation, as I see them,
are destined for greater success and distinction in
the teaching profession than were those of my
own.

This I believe to be true because of certain mental and emotional qualities common to the vast
majority of college women today, qualities resulting from this newest and most astonishing age in
which we live. Perhaps these new and astonishing young women actually possess no better capital for the present than we possessed for the past;
perhaps it is only time that has proved our "ancient good uncouth"; but it is pleasant and reas-
suring to think that an unstable world has created

a greater measure of stability in the best of its
young people.

Surely the girls whom I teach today are not only
more mature but vastly more intelligent than the
college students of thirty years ago. They are better balanced emotionally in that they are far less
sentimental. Their training in psychology and
philosophy has resulted in a far more objective
point of view, not only toward others but toward
themselves as well. They are much better informed
upon questions of current interest and importance
and much more alive to their individual responsibilities. They have a sense of humor too acute
to allow them to be fooled either by others or by
themselves; and their critical sense toward literature, music, the theatre, and other arts is, for the
most part, keen and extraordinarily sound. Finally,
because of the wise freedom of most modern college curriculums and because of the character and
personnel of the best college faculties today, they
are actually better educated and trained in the
subjects which they wish to teach than were college students a quarter of a century ago.

But, unlike me in 1909, they cannot be reasonably sure of a chance to use their talents and resources simply because there are not jobs enough
to go round. And if they wish to teach in the public schools of practically any state of the Union,
and in certain private schools as well, they are
required to spend a generous portion of their last

two years in college under the surveillance of Departments of Education, which, in accordance with State educational laws, supposedly prepare them for their class-rooms as they cannot otherwise be prepared. Such a requirement, as I see it, may tend to raise the level of mediocrity in public school teaching; but that it does much of anything for the girl who is cut out to be a good teacher, except to irritate her, I have yet to discover. Out of scores, even hundreds, of girls who have succumbed to the requirement and taken the courses, I have literally never discovered one who felt that they meant anything except a waste of good and valuable time.

The colleges of my day were not yet under the iron hands of State Boards of Education. If a girl wanted to teach English, history, Latin, or any other subject, she wisely took all the courses possible in the study of her choice and in others obviously related to it. In other words, she learned all that she could learn of the material which she was to teach, watched the teaching of it, decided which, if any, of her instructors she wished to emulate, and, when she set forth to teach, trusted to her own initiative, common sense, and enthusiasm to get across to her students what she herself had learned.

I wanted myself to teach English and history, and I prepared to do so by electing all possible courses in both together with Classics, which I still believe to be, in the original, or if the original is

impossible, in translation, the best possible training for a teacher of English. I took one course in
"Education" more out of curiosity than for any
other reason, the department having recently been
established at the university. I cannot believe I
learned from it anything of value to me in teaching, largely because my professors of history, English, and Classics were far better at their jobs than
was my professor of "Education," who suffered by
comparison. I also attended a course of lectures
entitled *The Organization and Administration of
Rural Schools,* a course given presumably because
so many college students of my day either inter-
rupted their four years to teach, as I had done, or
upon their graduation began their experience in
district schools. Since I had already with great
stress of mind and body organized and adminis-
tered two of these, and since the lecturer's theories
would have been worse than useless in Buck's Harbor, I decided early that I knew from rigorous
experience fully as much as he could teach me, if
not more.

It is doubtless for the good of our public school
systems that some training in the presentation of
subject matter should be given to prospective
teachers. But why it should be given at the sacri-
fice of a grounding in the subjects themselves and
why it should prove so extremely distasteful to
those who receive it, I have not been able to learn.

When I set out in the autumn of 1909 to discover

some high or private school sufficiently unen-
lightened to take a chance on me as a teacher, I
knew absolutely nothing of "Education" as it is
taught today. In place of it and its theories I had
had, thanks to my father, some forty weeks of
"practice teaching" under no supervision but my
own, if doubtless at some expense to my pupils.
Experience in a rural school wisely counted in
those days as good, if sometimes bitter, experience;
and a prospective high school teacher who had
weathered it was farther in line for a position
than those who had graduated from college with
no experience whatever.

Moreover, the University of Maine had during
my last two years, in consideration of my four
terms in a rural school, appointed me to a kind
of teaching fellowship, in return for which I
taught English to the students enrolled in a two
years' agricultural course. These boys came from
the farming districts of Maine and after two years
returned to them to farm their acres and raise their
stock more scientifically than they would otherwise
have known how to do. Most of them were high
school products, although some of them had had
only a "common school" education. Many of them
were older than I, and all of them were patient
and pleasant under my attempts to teach a subject of which they knew little and which seemed
to them comparatively useless.

I enjoyed my farmers and their themes on the

best manures for certain soils, on the breeding of stock, and on the future of Maine as a dairy state. They were one and all most decent young men, and they made up for what they lacked in externals in a stout ambition to get their money's worth. Even although they secretly saw little relation between the English grammar, the unity, coherence, and emphasis, which were then my stock in trade, and their lives on their Maine acres, they endured my ruthless enthusiasms with great good nature. At least they added not inconsiderably to my frail teaching experience and ensured me a better hope of a position once I had graduated from college.

The colleges and universities of those days did not maintain the machinery which they do today for the sake of connecting their graduates with the world of work. Vocational offices and appointment bureaus in their present state of efficiency were virtually unknown. Most teaching positions were obtained through membership in one or more of the scores of teachers' agencies scattered throughout the country; and the prospective teachers of my class in college joined these as a matter of course. We sent with our applications our photographs in cap and gown and any letters of recommendation which we had been able to extort from our professors. Then with not too many misgivings we waited for Destiny.

2

Unlike the other girls in my class who were bent on teaching I had joined an agency in Chicago known as the Clark Teachers' Agency. This ambitious and rather chimerical act had been suggested and encouraged by my professor of history, Caroline Colvin, who was an Indiana woman, trained in Bloomington. Had my father not known her and deeply respected her judgment and common sense, he would have relegated me with my classmates to the tender mercies of Fiske or Albert in Portland or in Boston and let it go at that. But after she had visited us in Blue Hill and somehow conveyed the impression that Mr. B. F. Clark of Chicago was eagerly awaiting my services, he had grudgingly given his consent.

To the average rural New Englander of thirty years ago and before the domination of the movies, the West was still a somewhat mythical region, populated by people most of whom had not had the good sense to stay at home. To my father the regions far beyond the Mississippi meant Bret Harte and Owen Wister's *The Virginian,* a book which he often read with as much pleasure as curiosity. This Far West was quite beyond my mother's interest and comprehension, but the Middle West of which Chicago was the horrible nucleus caused her no little anxiety when once she was acquainted with my vaulting ambition. In her bed-room there was a small wall cupboard which had contained as long as I could remember two strictly forbidden books. One was called *What Young Women Should Know* and the other, *If Christ Should Come to Chicago*. The contents of the first she had divulged to each of her daughters, when she felt the uneasy time had come, during an hour of acute embarrassment to her as well as to us. The contents of the second I had never seen except in hasty, forbidden glances until my mother raised the ban upon it in order to convince me that I should stay in Maine.

This odd book, bound in paper, pictured on its cover the Lord Himself approaching in a dejected mood the crowded buildings of a dark and presumably vicious city. It chronicled in heated language all the dens of vice which this city sheltered, all the greed and avarice which it personified; and my mother, a most intelligent woman in all other particulars, was moved by her anxiety and fear for my future to take some stock in it.

She was immensely relieved as the summer progressed with no favorable reply to the numberless applications which I had made for positions in Ohio, Indiana, and Illinois and of which Mr. Clark frequently informed me on impersonal pink slips. But when on a day in August a letter arrived for my father from my history professor, she was again made anxious and fearful. Miss Colvin wrote that she herself had seen Mr. B. F.

Clark, who felt that, could he but have me at close range, on the ground so to speak, a position would be immediately forthcoming. She offered the mad suggestion that I be allowed to come at once to Chicago where an acquaintance of hers would see that I was safely housed and where I should be in immediate proximity to Mr. Clark and to all the splendid positions which he held within his keeping.

I cannot give an adequate picture of the excitement, indeed, the consternation, into which this letter plunged my family. That I, who had only once seen Boston and who had never been beyond it except to attend a brief and completely chaperoned Y.W.C.A. conference at Lake George, should be begging to seek my own uncertain fortune in the Middle West was an unprecedented act of insubordination which grieved and bewildered my parents. I am sure I should never have been allowed to go had not an old family friend, now Chief Justice of the Maine Supreme Court, arrived in the teeth of my father's disapproval and on the very heels of his final refusal.

To Judge Charles Dunn of Orono I owe my entrance into a more multi-colored life than New England alone could have afforded me and to him I again accord my oft-repeated and perennial gratitude. He had been my friend from a child, for when I was five years old he had begun to read law with my father and had been as a young man for several years a member of our household. He thought Chicago and the Middle West in general not only the safest of places for me, but also an environment which from a financial point of view offered teachers far more than Maine could offer. This latter argument, I could see, appealed to my practical father; and after more arguments based on wider experience, responsibility, and larger opportunities for success than those afforded by New England, I could see with tense excitement that the day was won.

The following Sunday, after a week of frenzied preparation, the village photographer came to take our photographs as a united family, perhaps never again, my mother said, to be together; and on Monday I set forth to seek my fortune.

3

There is another way in which in August, 1909, I was more fortunate than young teachers today: I was younger in every respect than they can ever be. Indeed, no one in this year of grace, no matter from how simple an environment or from how small and undistinguished a college *could* be in as complete a state of blissful innocence of the world and its ways as was I as I set forth from Blue Hill upon my long journey. To be young, says Hazlitt, is to be as one of the immortals. It is doubtless true of any age and generation; and yet since youth at twenty-two is older now than I was at that age, the feeling of immortality is that much less intoxicating. Moreover, I was expectant as no girl of twenty-two in our present state of civilization can be expectant, surprised by literally everything I encountered, breathless with eagerness, consumed with ambition. Never so long as I live shall I forget the glowing, ecstatic sense of freedom, of power, which was mine as I boarded the train at Ellsworth, Maine, en route for Boston, the West, and my future. I was like those invincible ones in Isaiah as I waited upon my destiny. For I felt that I could run forever and not be weary, that I could walk forever in all manner of strange places and not faint.

My father had given me one hundred dollars in bills upon my departure. I am sure he had also given me excellent advice which I was in no state either to hear or to heed. He told me when he gave me the money that, since he had five other children to educate, this was his last provision for me. Any other sums which I might need, he said, he would be glad to furnish me at six per cent interest. This announcement, which cut me even further from my circumscribed past and set me fully upon my own feet, only added to my glorious sense of independence.

Ten dollars of my capital was in my purse; ninety was pinned closely within the pocket of my sister's brown suit, which, in a last gesture of supreme self-sacrifice, she had proffered me. I have always had an odd antipathy toward any shade of brown both as uninteresting and, to me, vastly unbecoming; but I do not believe that my appearance much dampened my ardor. In Boston some friends of my mother's saw me on the west-bound train quite as though I were departing for the Antipodes.

I had instructions in plenty, which had been given me through my history professor from her friend in Chicago. I was to stay in Chicago at a Bible Institute on the North Side, a place presumably well-designed to care for the young and inexperienced and of great assurance to my mother. When I reached the LaSalle Street Station, I was to pin a large handkerchief securely to the lapel of my coat and to look for an elderly gentleman with like insignia who would conduct me to the Bible Institute. Meanwhile there was the train itself tearing across Massachusetts, and there was I, still to my amazement, inside it.

I had never before travelled alone even on the briefest of journeys, never seen a Pullman car, never ordered and eaten a meal by myself. As we left Springfield and plunged onward through the Berkshire hills, already beginning to be touched with color, I thought I had never seen anything so beautiful. Little did I imagine at this moment so crammed and gleaming with the present that I should ever make my home among them! Yet

the world and everything in it were mine that
afternoon in a way baffling description; and were
I to name a day upon which merely to be alive
was enough, out of thousands of rich and abundant
days I should name that one in August thirty years
ago.

4

I was sitting up in my berth and peering
from the window the next morning long before
it was light enough to see. The flat expanse of
country, with the harvest already cut and with corn
stacked in golden huts upon the shorn ground, was
as fascinating to my eyes when it had once come
into vision as the tumbling Berkshire hills. It
made up in newness what it lacked in beauty. I
suddenly remembered how Stevenson in *Across
the Plains* had named as beautiful the words *Ohio,
Indiana, Illinois*. Now they seemed beautiful to
me also although I had never thought of them in
that way before.

When we at last swept through the sordid outskirts of Chicago in the early afternoon, I was
well-nigh exhausted even more from excitement
than from Middle Western heat. But my fervor
knew no lessening, and I pinned on one of my
father's large handkerchiefs in almost painful
curiosity and agitation. The elderly gentleman
promised by the Bible Institute was awaiting me,
similarly marked. I thought even then, I remem-

ber, that I should have recognized him without
his handkerchief since, among all the many persons on the platform, he alone could have emerged
from a Bible Institute.

He conducted me with a benevolent and, I felt,
faintly disapproving air to the elevated railroad,
and I staggered after him bearing my suit-case,
which he did not offer to carry and which I was
too embarrassed to give to any importuning porter, not being sure of them and their ways. Once
we had landed within the Bible Institute and I
had been shown my very hot and somewhat musty
room, I decided that benevolence and faint disapproval were two of the current attitudes of
that institution. By the time I had eaten my supper in company with others of its inmates, I had
added to these, suspicion and a very unattractive
zeal.

My mother was quite right in assuming that I
should be safe within its doors. Surely no one
would enter it who was not compelled by inner
or by outer force to do so! It was a place devoted
to one purpose, namely the saving of souls, and
even to me, whose religious background had been
extremely simple, not to say fervent at times, it
was the most embarrassing of hostels. All the dozen
or so young women whom it housed were training
to be evangelists, as I learned to my great confusion at supper when two of them asked me if I
had made the great decision. Upon my vowing

hastily and stoutly that I had, their suspicion of me somewhat relaxed for the moment, but their zeal was fired to anecdotal vigor by their very relief.

I stayed two weeks in the Bible Institute. It was the only place I have ever known which grew increasingly unpalatable from constant association. I never quite knew whether to admire or to dislike the single-minded young women, who, when they were not at prayer, at oral testimonials, or at Bible study, went about doing good; but I think my only genuine emotion toward them and their activities was an extreme sense of embarrassment. We never had quite enough to eat, I remember, although perhaps my hunger partly resulted from the uncomfortable knowledge that everyone but me was dedicated to the principle that man does not live by bread alone. Before we sat down to each scanty meal, we sang a hymn with a chorus which said,

"O be nothing, nothing!"

Since I had come to Chicago with the express purpose of being something, I found this hymn exceedingly irritating. I think I regarded it with superstition as well, fearing that the thrice-daily repetition of its refrain might result in my becoming precisely nothing at all!

We had nightly prayer circles at which my presence was tacitly expected and my habitual silence the cause of renewed suspicion. This atmosphere of constant petition with which the entire establishment was redolent got somewhat on my nerves, not to say my conscience, especially since the only praying of which I was capable throughout the fortnight was of a most selfish and anti-social nature, namely that I might get a job.

Had I not, indeed, like St. Paul been intent only upon "this one thing", had I not been tormented by fears lest I should fail therein, I might conceivably have become interested in the Bible Institute and in the study of its strange, tenacious, fervid minds. But the more intent I became upon my own future as the jobless days went on, the more its curious existence seemed a law unto itself and quite divorced from life outside its grimy, comfortless walls. I learned, however, that it was known elsewhere. For when Mr. B. F. Clark, the manager of the teachers' agency which held my future in its hands, asked me upon the occasion of my first call upon him where I was living in Chicago, and I told him, he rose from his chair and cried, "My God!"

5

I shall always remember my first visit to Mr. Clark's office in Steinway Hall on Van Buren Street. He told me some years afterwards that he remembered it, too, in fact that it had always stood him in good stead as a source of amusement when he needed entertainment in his thoughts. I am sure that no young teacher from Maine had ever before journeyed jobless to Chicago to cast herself upon his mercy. I am sure, too, that he was quite unprepared to meet such eager ingenuousness in a young woman, even in those days when artlessness was still not uncommon among the young.

I went to see him the first morning after my arrival in Chicago, when I had ascertained from the most worldly of the Bible students how I should get to Van Buren Street. I went on the street-car since I did not dare essay the elevated railroad by myself, and I carried my suit-case with me. I do not know just why I thus encumbered myself. Perhaps I was still conscious of my mother's adjurations to keep my most valuable possessions with me as much as possible in such a city. But I think rather that I needed a generous receptacle for more letters of recommendation and for the themes which I had written in college and which, I thought, might give added proof to Mr. Clark that I knew something about the teaching of English.

When I had once reached Van Buren Street with my suit-case and had taken the elevator to the eleventh floor of Steinway Hall, I was in a frightful state of nervous excitement, which did not lessen upon my discovery that no one of a dozen young women in a dozen different offices had ever so much as heard of me. After a long wait during which the furious beating of my heart sent added blood to my already very red cheeks, I was, however, ushered, still with my suit-case, into the presence of him upon whose probably long since forgotten suggestion I had come to Chicago. Mr. Clark, seeing my suit-case, quite naturally thought I had only just arrived; and when I explained that it contained documents which might be of interest to him, he leaned back in his chair and laughed long and loudly.

He was a small, round man of perhaps fifty, with intensely blue round eyes set in a very smooth, pink face. He had brushy white hair parted in the middle, and he was dressed in a light gray suit with a red tie. As I stood there much embarrassed before him, I thought of George Meredith, who had recently died and who, I had read somewhere, favored light gray suits with red ties. For a moment I thought self-consciously of impressing Mr. Clark by the comparison and then thought better of it.

I asked instead whether he really thought I should get a position, and I remember that he said he felt sure of it, since he could not allow some school to be deprived of me. I took this as a compliment at the moment and felt much encouraged, although later I realized that another meaning lurked within his words. My heart leaped at his next announcement.

"Let me see," he said. "There may be something

this minute. What about Mason City, Iowa? They want a Latin teacher."

My heart fell as quickly as it had risen.

"I'm afraid Iowa is beyond the Mississippi, isn't it?" I said.

"Why the Mississippi?" asked Mr. Clark, fumbling among other papers on his desk. "It's a nice river. Got anything against it?"

"No," said I. "It's only that my mother would prefer me not to go beyond the Mississippi unless it's really necessary."

Mr. Clark laughed again. I could see that our interview was unusual to him in many respects. Then he told me with great encouragement that he felt reasonably sure some opening this side of the Mississippi would put in an appearance before many days had passed. I in turn assured him that with his permission I should look in at the office every morning at this hour, and he did not seem to object to my proposal.

6

The morning of my first visit to Mr. Clark is also memorable to me because of a somewhat terrifying as well as humorous accident which befell me before I was again safely within the walls of the Bible Institute. There is always, I think, an element of pathos in inexperience and the mishaps which it often calls down upon itself, humorous as such mishaps may be. Perhaps for this very reason much of the humor of today lacks a kind of mellowness since inexperience has become so relatively impossible in an age like our own.

I had lived all of my twenty-two years in the country and in the most countrified country at that. The college which I attended was a country college, situated in a small town, the nearest city being the inconsiderable one of Bangor. I knew nothing of great cities and their ways, and had I not been so eager to enjoy my new freedom to its limit and to learn all that I could about my new surroundings, I should have felt terrified by Chicago, its dirt, its uproar, and its frenzied rush.

Strange and frightening as everything seemed to me, however, I determined upon leaving Mr. Clark's office on Van Buren Street to walk to the Bible Institute. I was impelled to do so by a variety of desires: to make my next letter home as dramatic and interesting as possible; to see what Chicago was really like; to avoid another street-car since in the first I had felt extremely self-conscious and ill at ease; and above all else to postpone as long as possible my re-entry into the Bible Institute. Even with my suit-case the distance did not seem long to me when the impatient door-man at Steinway Hall had explained to me with many pointings of a scornful finger the requisite blocks west and the turn northward.

I reached Dearborn Street with no disaster and

turned northward. The day was warm, and I took my time, seemingly the only person, I thought, on the street who was not in a hurry. There was and still is, unless I am mistaken, a bridge on Dearborn Street which crosses the Chicago River. The structure of this bridge meant nothing to me, but I lingered thereon, being fascinated by the filthy water of the river and by a peculiar craft coming upstream. This struck me, I remember, as odd since there was obviously no way by which it might proceed beyond the bridge. I walked on slowly, studying the steady progress of the boat, when I was startled by the blowing of whistles and the apparent haste of everyone but me. Whether I was hidden by the iron uprights of the bridge from the sight of the men responsible for its manipulation, I do not know; but by the time I had come to my senses and was hurrying to reach the other side, I felt to my horror the solid boards beneath my feet begin to rise in the air and to place me and my suit-case in an ever-increasingly precarious position at an angle of some forty-five degrees.

Terrified as I was at this angle, which, I surmised, must steadily increase toward ninety degrees, I had sense enough now to realize quickly the connection between the bridge and the boat. Since the bridge had parted in its middle and was rising in the air to allow the passage of the boat, I knew that it was destined to come down again. I had not come to Chicago to meet my death, and I instantly decided upon the only way to avoid it. I wedged my suit-case between two of the iron supports which met at an angle and somehow cast myself upon it with my arms clinging to whatever there was to cling to. I would hold on, I determined, with all my strength until the bridge once again assumed its normal position, when I would extricate myself and walk off with what dignity I could muster.

But by the time my decisions were made and I was placed in my desperate position, the men in charge of this curious feat of engineering had spotted me. There were shouts, more blowing of whistles, the gathering of a crowd on the nearer bank of the river. The boat backed downstream; the bridge began to descend. I felt it slowly dropping backward behind me. It clanged and bumped into position; and I was lifted to my feet by two policemen who had run onto the bridge from the nearer pavement.

Once on the street I found myself the center of a strange assortment of men and women, many with foreign faces, who, used to such bridges as this, had been awaiting its normal behavior in order to cross the river. I instantly recognized that my courage in the face of danger meant nothing whatever to them. They thought I was either mad or senseless and were curiously waiting to discover which.

The bigger policeman, who had not relinquished his hold upon me, began at once to question me.

"Young woman," he screamed, "are you tired of life? Just what do you mean by not heeding signals?"

I explained as best I could, while the crowd increased and I wanted terribly to die, that I had never before seen such a bridge and that I had not understood the connection between the signals and myself.

"Will you kindly tell us," asked the other policeman, who still held my suit-case, looking upon it occasionally with disdain and scorn, "who you are and where on earth you hail from?"

I strove to hold back my nervous tears as I gave my name and the state of my kindly engendure, which at that moment I devoutly wished I had never left.

The crowd howled with unkind amusement and repeated the howl when, upon further harsh inquiry, I was obliged to tell where I was staying in the city. I thought for some terrible moments that I was not to be allowed to proceed on my way unattended by the law; but my obvious innocence and the sight of my tears apparently convinced the policemen that I was truthful, if a fool, and they at last let me go.

A kind-faced woman walked five blocks with me. She insisted upon carrying my suit-case, and, although I could not speak a word to her, I have always felt toward her a gratitude which I have felt toward few persons before or since.

The Bible Institute for the only time during my stay in Chicago looked good to me when I had once reached it. I hurried to my room to burst into tears of utter humiliation upon my miserable bed. For days I suffered paroxysms of dread lest my exploit appear in the papers and reach the round, blue eyes of Mr. Clark, who would then and there decide that such ignorance deserved no confidence. But apparently, I concluded, when I again felt safe, it was of importance only as a story to be told as a joke by all the strange and awful people who had witnessed it.

It was months before I saw that it had its humorous aspects, not, indeed, until it had been received with high amusement by friends whom I was soon to make. Most of them, I think, never really believed the story in spite of my asseverations. But it was so true in every detail that it even now reappears in certain dreams of terror. For when in the night I find myself, like De Quincey, jeered at by monsters in human form, I know that far back somewhere in my mind the Dearborn Street bridge still stands, flanked by Chinamen and negroes and two burly policemen, and that I, even in my sleep, am searching somewhere for a kind-faced woman to thank her after many years.

7

I have often since wondered exactly what I did during that fortnight in Chicago. I think it was a period not of action so much as of certain concentrated and extremely limited states of mind. I was too beset by fear and uncertainty to read much, as I should otherwise have done. My bodily frame attended prayer circles and went occasionally under the chaperonage of the elderly gentleman with the handkerchief to hysterical, revivalistic gatherings in certain undesirable portions of the city; but my mind rarely accompanied it. I am sure I walked miles on bridgeless streets and along the Lake front, hopeful at times, at others fearful. I grew thin during that fortnight, partly from scanty, ill-cooked meals, mostly from anxiety.

But at last on an afternoon early in September Mr. Clark summoned me to Van Buren Street, and I went in a fever of excitement. He said, while I stood opposite him trembling with hope, that a certain school in Wisconsin had been so favorably impressed by a letter concerning me that its headmistresses wished to see me. They wanted a teacher of history who would assist in English. Above everything else they wanted one who knew and liked the country. The school, Mr. Clark said, was a rather unusual boarding-school known as the Hillside Home School; and although its mistresses preferred a teacher with more experience than mine, he thought it might afford the very place for me. He said that with my approval he would inform the Lloyd-Jones sisters that I would arrive at Spring Green, Wisconsin, which was the nearest town to Hillside, on the following afternoon at six o'clock.

I presume I walked back to the Bible Institute on ordinary pavements, but they were to me high and wide pathways toward my future. The dirty city which had terrified and humiliated me seemed clothed in light, shining and kind. I caught myself smiling at strangers on the street who, surprised, smiled shyly back at me. I was now freed from anxiety and fear, for in my new resiliency I had not a doubt in my mind that, whoever the Lloyd-Jones sisters were, they were as eagerly awaiting me as I was awaiting them. This assurance prompted me to pack my trunk before supper so that, when I was once engaged to teach at the Hillside Home School, I might not have to return to Chicago at all. I would then, I thought, write the Bible Institute to send it after me so that I might never again have to climb its steps to peal its clanging, dissonant bell.

I remember that at supper that night I asked boldly for another piece of cake and a second helping of custard. The horrified silence which greeted my request was broken at last by the most serious of the would-be evangelists, who offered me her portion, which she assured me she did not want. I do not think I even demurred at accepting it or blushed at my temerity. For I was leaving this odd house where the desire of everyone was to be nothing and embarking on my way where I was to be something at last.

THE HILLSIDE HOME SCHOOL

IV

WHEN at twilight the next day I stepped from the train at Spring Green, Wisconsin, uneasiness had again begun to assail me. My four hours' journey through shorn yellow fields and rolling dark hills had convinced me that I wanted to stay in country like this. The very fact that I felt so much at home created new anxiety. Conceivably the Lloyd-Jones sisters would not be attracted by me from Maine, my youth, and my relative inexperience. I was worried over my generous portion of the dirt and soot from the train and by the absence of a button which had somehow escaped from my brown suit and was apparently gone for good.

I was met by a kind-faced man with very dark eyes and a long white beard. He told me that he was Enos Lloyd-Jones, that he managed the school farm for his sisters, and that he was to drive me to Hillside some three miles toward the west. Whatever appearance of age he had possessed at my first sight of him was dispelled as we drove from the town and into the country behind a fine pair of horses. He had a pleasing voice and spoke as though he had respect for his own words. I liked him so much at once that I was impelled to confidence upon his asking me why and when I had come from Maine and how long I had been in Chicago. He was vastly amused and, I thought, a bit saddened by the Bible Institute and wished I had instead stayed with his brother, Jenkin Lloyd-Jones, who, he said, was a Unitarian minister and the head of an establishment called Lincoln Center for work among the poor.

The country which we drove through was beautiful in the early evening light. The Wisconsin River which we crossed had through centuries past cut a wide valley for itself, leaving dark hills beyond. Three of these hills, he told me, as we approached them, turned and followed their clear outlines, were called by Welsh names, Bryn Mawr, Bryn Canol, and Bryn Bach, or Big, Middle, and Little Hill. Lloyd-Jones was itself a Welsh name. His father and mother had come to Wisconsin from Cardiganshire in Wales in 1845. They had settled in this valley with five sons and five daughters before the close of the Civil War. The sons, like their father, with the exception of Jenkin, the preacher, were farmers and owned most of the land at Hillside.

I could see the darkening farms with their open fields dotted here and there with cattle, their great barns and silos, their comfortable houses, lying in the shadow of the hills, east and west, south and north, as we turned from Bryn Mawr, Bryn Canol, and Bryn Bach and drove through the valley. We crossed a stream with willows and, making another sharp turn toward the right, drove up a steep incline and stopped before a large, gray-shingled house, the Home Building, I was told, through the lighted windows of which I could see a fire blazing. Uncle Enos, as he said I should call him, helped me from the carriage and led me indoors. There was a small table by the fire spread for my supper. He said the "aunts", who, I gathered, were his sisters, were at a family supper at his farm across the way but would come home early to see me. I shall always remember him as he stood in the doorway with his large white straw hat in his hand and his white head and beard against the entrance light. He looked patriarchal as he stood there, kind, too, solid and substantial. But I fear that in my egoism I remember him most distinctly at that moment because he said that he hoped I would stay at Hillside. I hoped so, too, as, after I had seen my room and made myself as presentable as possible, I sat down to my supper before the fire.

2

I was pretending to read when Ellen and Jane Lloyd-Jones walked into the living-room at eight o'clock. I might have been prepared for them from having seen their brother, but I was not; in fact, during the three years I lived and worked with them, they always took me by surprise and left me in wonder. They were tall, stately women, rather small of frame, certainly not large. They had the same snow-white hair of their brother, but whereas Jane's was curly and without gloss, Ellen's was straight and shining. I do not know their age exactly. Ellen was the older, somewhere in the early sixties, I suppose, and Jane three or four years younger. Their eyes were very dark, Ellen's a deep brown, Jane's as nearly black as eyes can be. It was easy to see at the first glance that the older was a bit less vivid than the younger, more gentle of nature, more lacking in vitality. Alone she would have seemed, as she was, rich in nature; in comparison, she was less startling. One supplemented the other in a curious manner, even upon first acquaintance. I was later to understand how together they gave the warmth and the fire, the stability and the strength, the soul and the spirit which for nearly thirty years sustained and supported the most wholesome and abundant of schools.

I felt more shy and young than I had ever felt, I think, as they walked into the room and greeted me. Their height and dignity made me seem small and graceless. The gracious, book-lined room and their equally gracious presence within it seemed suddenly out of place in the silence of the country outside the house, at variance with barns and cattle and rich, black soil. In their silk gowns standing there, one in lavender, the other in pale gray, they belonged, I thought, to some more elegant setting than a Wisconsin valley, perhaps, I thought, to a salon in Paris or to the opera in Vienna.

They sat down at once and began to talk with me. Ellen did far more of the talking than did her sister; and yet I felt uncomfortably sure that it was Jane who would make the decision as to whether or not I should stay at Hillside. As Ellen talked, Jane fussed at the already brilliant fire with a long, three-pronged fork. In spite of my trepidation her hands fascinated me. They were nervous brown hands with exceptionally long and slender fingers. She did not look at me at all, although now and then she put in a brisk question.

They surprised me by not asking anything about what I knew in the subjects for which they needed a teacher. They wanted to know instead if I liked the country, if children amused and interested me, if I liked and could take long walks, if I should not greatly miss the sea should I come to live among the hills, if I knew anything about birds and common flowers. I could see that they were favorably impressed when I told them that I could walk indefinitely and that I knew all the familiar New England birds and many of the Maine flowers. Jane rose from her chair then and rummaged in the table drawer for some plates of Wisconsin birds, not known or uncommon in Maine, the red-headed woodpecker, the scarlet tanager, and the meadow-lark. She told me then of a flock of evening grosbeaks, which had come the preceding winter for the first time since she was a child, and how the whole school had been dismissed to see them, golden against the snow. It was easy to see that the flock of grosbeaks weighed more heavily in her mind than even the English grammar which, if I came, I should have to teach. They asked me if I liked animals, if I rode and liked horses. They wanted to know about my family in Maine, my many brothers and sisters, of the number of which I could see they approved. They asked me what I liked most among books and if I knew and loved music, my confessed ignorance of which I could see disappointed them. They were vastly amused and, I thought, favorably impressed by my venturing from Maine to the Middle West to seek my fortune.

We talked until ten o'clock. When they had finished their investigation of me, they told me about their school, which seemed to me the most unique and delightful of schools. Then we went into a huge, clean kitchen and foraged about for milk and crackers. Perhaps this bedtime repast before the fire with its pleasant, friendly atmosphere decided them to put my anxiety at rest; perhaps they had had a hurried colloquy in the pantry while I waited in the kitchen; for just before we ascended the stairs to bed, Jane informed me that they thought I would do for the Hillside Home School and that they would be very glad to have me stay on for the fortnight before its opening.

When we reached the second floor, Jane said good night and went at once down a long corridor to her room at its end. Her sister went into my room with me and, to my surprise, turned down my bed for me before she bade me good night. She told me as she left that she and her sister were always called Aunt Nell and Aunt Jennie by all their children in the school as well as by their teachers; and she suggested that I begin these friendly salutations at once.

3

I suppose that the Hillside Home School, were it existing today exactly as it was existing in 1909, would be termed a progressive school by all the supporters and disciples of such institutions. Yet the charm and value of Hillside lay in the fact that it did not stand off and gaze complacently at itself as a pioneer in the new education. In other words, it lacked the self-consciousness as well as the self-righteousness of certain of our modern experiments in child growth instead of child discipline. Hillside was too busy doing its job to define itself in pedagogical terms. It was simply a school, a home, and a farm all in one, and the contribution and strength of each element lay in the fact that each was never separated from the other.

Ten years before Mr. John Dewey at the University of Chicago "ignited the flame of the current educational revolution", fourteen years before Colonel Francis Parker lent his name to what he termed *child-centered* education, and a full quarter of a century before the progressive school as we know it was springing up from Massachusetts to California, this school in a remote Wisconsin valley was looking upon each child as an individual and centering all its efforts on his reasonable growth, activity, and self-expression. Hillside did not do this because its headmistresses had discovered something new and untried. They were instead utilizing old virtues in education, too little used, perhaps, but surely as old as when Socrates sat down to talk with young Phaedrus about the nature of love and the soul under plane trees by the river Ilissus instead of in an Athenian house of learning. They were utilizing these virtues of sympathy, understanding, patience, wisdom, and humor simply because they were sympathetic, understanding, patient, wise, and humorous women. Too many "educators" today insist that the failure of what they term the old education lay in its wrong approach to children, its wrong methods, its inflexible systems. What they apparently fail to see is that the failure of any education, old or new, lies openly and, one would think, obviously, not in approach or in method but in the personality and character of those who teach. No method or lack of it can ever dim human vision and understanding; nor can all the methods or approaches of all the teachers' colleges in the universe in the slightest measure supply what was left out of certain teachers upon the day they were born.

Ellen and Jane Lloyd-Jones would have been perplexed as well as highly amused had they known of the existence of such pretentious terms as *orientation, integration, behavior patterns, units of work, adjustments to environment, a socialized atmosphere,* and *the rhythmic basis of life.* They did not need to talk of *the law of self-activity,* for they had recognized and encouraged it since they had begun their school as the only reasonable and decent way to treat a child. Their school had quite naturally grown out of themselves. It was human because they were human, kind because they were kind, sensible because they were themselves the epitome of common sense. Hillside was not an experiment, and because it was not it was unencumbered either by self-consciousness or by argument and agitation. I am sure it never occurred to Ellen or to Jane Lloyd-Jones that their notion of children and of their wholesome upbringing needed either explanation or defense. Hillside was merely a way of life, sound, reasonable, co-operative, and enchanting.

Ellen and Jane Lloyd-Jones were of Welsh stock. They came from a long line of farmers, preachers, and teachers in Cardiganshire. Their father and mother, Richard and Mary Thomas Lloyd-Jones, had come to America in 1844, to Wisconsin in 1845. They brought with them three sons and three daughters, Thomas, John, and Jenkin, Margaret, Mary, and Anna. On their Wisconsin farm in Ixonia were born Ellen, Jane, James, and Enos.

Before the end of the Civil War, as Uncle Enos had told me, the family had established itself at Hillside. The valley was virtually its own, as Richard Lloyd-Jones with his strong Welsh love of home and family had chosen this rich and pleasant site because it provided farms for his sons as well as for himself. In the shadow of the hills about rose the barns, silos, and homes of Thomas, James, John, and Enos. In 1887 when Hillside Home School was founded these tall farmers were known to the first children at the new school as Uncle Thomas, Uncle James, Uncle John, and Uncle Enos.

Ellen and Jane Lloyd-Jones in 1887 gave up responsible positions as teachers to found their school. The former had been head of the department of history in the River Falls State Normal School in Wisconsin; the latter had been director of kindergarten training-schools in St. Paul, Minnesota. The idea of a school at Hillside had its initial conception in the desire to provide good teaching, which should include sound preparation for college, for their many nieces and nephews and for the other country children of near-by neighborhoods. It was extended before the actual building of the school to include any children elsewhere in city or country whose parents might be interested in a country boarding-school.

From its opening in September, 1887, the Hillside School was an integral part of the life in the valley. The uncles and aunts on the neighboring farms, their lawns, gardens, homes, and fields, their horses and their cattle, were familiarly known to every child of every age. When the nephews and nieces grew to college age and went from Hillside to the university at Madison or elsewhere throughout the country, many to become themselves well known in various capacities, their parents remained uncles and aunts to succeeding scores and hundreds of boys and girls, who ran in and out of their houses, watched and helped them in their farming, and loved them because they were worthy of it.

From the beginning the heads of this new and unique school had planned for the education and wholesome nurture of both boys and girls of every age from five to eighteen. Since to them a school meant, first and foremost, a family, they could not think of limiting and crippling their family either by no boys or by no girls. Upon the site of their farm-house and their own childhood home they erected a large and pleasant house known always as the Home Building. This was designed as a home for girls from thirteen to eighteen. The original house which Richard Lloyd-Jones had built they moved a short distance away, named it Home Cottage, and used it as a home for younger girls. They built another small house, beneath the shadow of the northern hill behind the school. This they called West Cottage, and there small boys were placed. Older boys of high school age had their own homelike dormitory near by. In 1903 this was connected with an adequate and beautiful school building of native limestone, designed and erected by Frank Lloyd Wright, the son of Anna Lloyd-Jones and a nephew of Ellen and Jane.

These buildings were built or appropriated in the early years of the school as the need arose. By the time ten years had passed, this healthful and lovely valley in Wisconsin had become known throughout the Middle West and farther away not only as a place where children were sure to be well and to receive the best of training, but also as a home where under reasonable discipline and supervision both boys and girls might realize the best of which they were capable in physical and mental, emotional and spiritual growth.

4

Few young teachers at any period have been, or can ever be, more blessed than I by the environment and the objectives of their first schools. To few has Destiny been so charitable and far-seeing. I should never have done at that time for a school in the city. I knew too little of city children or of city parents on their own ground. I should have been ill at ease and, therefore, inadequate before associates with more sophistication and far more urban advantages than I had had. Hillside for me, among other manifold riches, was the best of stepping-stones. Most of the other teachers there, although all of them knew and loved the country, had been bred in larger centers, educated in better-known and more distinguished colleges than mine. They had travelled; they knew more than a little of art, of music, and the theatre, of the ways of the world as I did not. Through the common medium of the country, of which I knew perhaps more than they, they could quite unconsciously teach me things that I did not know and open hitherto closed doors to wider, more cultural experience. Surely the lines fell unto me in pleasant places!

For three years I lived and worked at Hillside; yet no inadequate words of mine can catch or record its atmosphere or accurately explain just what it was to both teachers and children. It combined, as I have said before, a farm, a school, and

a home. This trinity of indivisible interests was in
every sense a unity. The barns and barnyards and
all that went on within them were open to the children at all times as were the fields and pastures.
No team of horses went to work on Saturday
mornings unaccompanied by half a dozen boys of
various ages. Boys likewise were allowed by good-
humored hired men to care for the horses in the
barns, to learn to milk if they wished. The cows and
horses at Hillside were members of the family,
each known by name, each respected and liked.
Children whose parents could afford it were encouraged to keep their ponies or horses at school,
and, needless to say, they cared for these themselves.

The warm southern slope of the rise behind the
school was laid out each spring in small gardens.
There was hardly a boy or a girl of any age who
did not want a garden of his own, even although
ownership entailed complete responsibility for the
care of it from early spring to closing time. The
school table depended upon these gardens for
early lettuce, carrots, and radishes; and children
vied with one another in competing for the first
edible crop. Seeds or plants were selected and
bought by oneself from one's own pocket money.
Some ambitious boys bought strawberry plants
and raised their berries from year to year with
care, intelligence, and pride. The sandy soil in
spots was good for melons, and boys said good-bye

to their melon patches in the early summer with careful and detailed instructions to farm-hands for their care until September. To go home from Hillside for the summer vacation, however, was no unalterable law. Boys and girls whose parents for one reason or another found it difficult or unwise to have them at home might stay at Hillside through the holidays also, attend to their own melon patches, work and play about the farm.

The presence of country boys and girls who came from neighboring farms as day scholars provided an additional interest in the farming aspects of Hillside. Perhaps a third of the school was made up of this wholesome country product. That they were liked and admired by their school companions from the city and that their houses, barns, and even supper-tables always gave welcome to Hillside in general, spoke well for the sense of values characteristic of our community.

Both of the aunts were authorities on Wisconsin birds, and from its beginning the school had taken the knowledge and enjoyment of familiar birds as a matter of course. In the early spring mornings children went by themselves or with their teachers to the river on the hunt for red-wings, to a certain clump of box-elders on Thomas Ridge which scarlet tanagers were known to frequent, to certain thickets where brown thrushes and towhees were almost bound to be. The sight of the first red-winged blackbird in the spring, or of any other

migratory bird, was an event at Hillside. The boy
or girl who had first seen it was allowed to enter
his name, the time and the place, on the bird chart
in the school hall.

It was the same with flowers. The native anem-
one, or pasque flower, of Wisconsin was the first
blossom to appear on sunny southern hillsides;
and hordes of sharp-eyed children after three
o'clock ranged the countryside to be the first to
bring back his glory and honor to one or the other
of the aunts. The decoration of the tables in the
long, bright dining-room was given week by week
into the keeping of certain boys and girls. On some
unusually fair and sunny morning in May school
was dismissed before it was opened, and all of us
trooped to the Three Hills on the sides of which
field violets grew in lavish profusion. These were
picked literally in thousands and tens of thousands, brought back home and re-made into
bunches by us all. They were then packed in
great flat containers and sent off by the afternoon
train to hospitals in Madison and Chicago.

Botany at Hillside meant field trips upon one's
own. Not only flowers but weeds and ferns were
recognized and classified. The habits and traits of
common trees were known by being familiarly
talked about. The various varieties of wingéd
seeds in the spring were matters of deep interest
to us all. I quickly learned why the aunts wanted
no teachers who did not love the country. Such a

one would have been miserable, out of place, and useless at Hillside. But in the three years I was there, there was no such dull and undesirable person roundabout.

In the fall we had a nut-gathering day, going on foot, on horseback, or in farm-wagons to the hickory and black walnut groves. In the winter, on some clear and snowy morning when it was not too cold, it was announced at breakfast that the day seemed made for the winter ride and that we would best lose no time in getting off. There were five or six great sledges of us bound for some place twenty miles or so away which could provide us with dinner. There were bells on the horses and a wonderful sense of freedom and exhilaration as we slid over the country roads, around and through the snowy hills. It is pleasant to think that there are hundreds of men on farms and in offices in any number of places who will never forget the Hillside winter ride, and hundreds of women who, remembering it, will puzzle over the ways and means of bringing up sons and daughters as wholesomely as Hillside brought hers up with, apparently, never a problem at all.

The well-defined boundaries of the valley, the uniformity, simplicity, and stability of its people, were naturally responsible in a large degree for the triumph of Hillside; and yet these values might have lain undiscovered and useless as contributions to a school had the founders of that school been other than what they were. Ellen and Jane Lloyd-Jones were themselves country children. They realized as they grew older the infinite resources for the nourishment and cultivation of the human mind and imagination which such a condition of life may hold within itself if only its potentialities are understood. The Lloyd-Joneses one and all had within themselves, in their appearance and speech, in their humor and insight, in the simplicity and strength of their thinking, all the abundant riches of their own environment, and these riches they gave to every child and to every teacher who came under their care and into their association.

5

When I think of Hillside and give back to it the appreciation of many years, I think of it, first of all, at its meal-times. Then all its features of the best and wisest of homes were apparent. The dining-room was a large room with many windows. There were in my time some eight tables, each seating ten or twelve. A teacher sat at either end of a table, and along its sides were boys and girls of all ages, so interspersed that big and little were alternated. Some youngster of five, or six, or seven was invariably placed next a boy or girl of sixteen or eighteen so that his manners might be noted and his wants supplied by a watchful elder. This responsibility for small children was always tacitly placed upon older ones and as tacitly undertaken. I do not remember anything ever being said about it.

There were, in fact, fewer rules at Hillside than in any school I have ever known. The spirit of co-operation was its one standard; the avoidance of behavior uncomfortable and embarrassing to others was seemingly its ruling principle. These were not so much set forth as precepts as they were inspired by example. Ill-mannered, ill-adjusted children soon found that they were unhappy because they were conspicuous. If they were reproved, they were quite as often reproved by their fellows as by their teachers.

Before each meal at Hillside grace was said. This ceremony was allotted to each table in turn, and also in turn to every member of it whatever his age. Each, moreover, was responsible for the form of his words. He might recite a prayer, the stanza of a hymn, a verse from the Bible, or a short poem which he liked and had learned for that good reason. We had an infinite variety of graces; but a common understanding of the seriousness and responsibility of the moment demanded that no invocation, whatever its content, be laughed at.

Our meals at Hillside were the most pleasant of occasions. There was nothing whatever about them that savored of an institution, even of a school. The family atmosphere banished any other idea.

Sometimes Aunt Nell read to us at supper from her central table in the window recess. Very often she told us news that concerned the family: something exciting which had happened in the barns, plans for some special occasion. When she rose from her chair, we always knew that something interesting was forthcoming, and every table ceased its clatter on the instant.

The family atmosphere was increased after supper on every night except Sunday, for we always read aloud in groups for an hour. Aunt Jennie read to the boys of high-school age in her room, Aunt Nell to the girls of the same age in hers. The middle-sized and younger children were read to by the teachers in charge of their respective cottages. For two years I had seven little girls in Home Cottage who never wanted to go to bed once we had begun *The Secret Garden, Sara Crewe,* or *Children of the New Forest.*

Life at Hillside required initiative, versatility, humor, and sound common sense. More than once I decided that my English and history classes were really only my avocation; for after my first year there I was a mother almost more than I was a teacher. During my first year I lived on the third floor of the Home Building as companion to eight or nine girls of high-school age. At the beginning of my second year I was placed in charge of Home Cottage with a family of seven small girls and of one small boy of five, who was thought to be too

young for the steady companionship of boys ten or
twelve. My youngsters thus varied in age from five
to twelve: three of eight years old, one of ten, two
of eleven, and one awkward child of twelve, who
had the ear-ache in the winter seemingly four
nights out of seven.

There was an efficient German housekeeper at
Hillside named Fräulein Schultz, an energetic,
forthright woman, who had most definite ideas as
to where her responsibility began and more especially as to where it stopped. She did not think
minor household catastrophes any concern of hers.
This stand resulted quite naturally, since we had
no resident nurse, in the development of diverse
resources in the teachers. Hands at Hillside were
quite as valuable as heads when occasion demanded
them; and there were many days when I went to
my classes feeling that they were at best an interruption in my family life.

I shall never forget one disastrous and funny
week following the spring holidays in my second
year. The children had returned to school as irri-
table, tired, and physically upset as children invariably are after an indulgent vacation at home.
One of my eight-year-olds, whose home was in
Chicago, began a furious scratching of her head
immediately upon her return. The teacher who
was with me in Home Cottage, presumably to assist me in the care of the children, was a charming,
absent-minded girl who knew far more about good

music than about the possible cause of violent
scratching of one's head. Although she had always
inspected and sometimes arranged the child's hair
each morning before our progress to breakfast, she
had discovered nothing amiss; and by the time the
situation had been brought to my horrified attention, the inhabitants of Janet's heavy curls were
well settled, increasing and multiplying.

When I sought out Fräulein Schultz for counsel
and assistance, she summarily informed me that
heads and their occupants were not within her
province. She did, however, commend soft soap
and kerosene and after supplying both these in-
gredients left me to my own devices. After the first
vigorous application Janet sat in her room all day
with a turkish towel over her head, and I taught
a Shakespearean tragedy to a vastly amused class
with all the windows open.

That very afternoon three others of my household complained of itching in a different locality
and upon examination I discovered the same rash
on all three. Knowing too well the temperament
of Fräulein Schultz, I sought out Uncle Enos,
who suggested that we take one child as a sample
to the local doctor in Spring Green. This versatile
old man pronounced the malady common, old-
fashioned itch and sent me home with a generous
package of sulphur which he ordered mixed with
lard and rubbed into all three patients for three
nights running. He further suggested a rubbing of

all remaining children in my household with alcohol as a preventative.

I had a busy time that evening with eight naked children to be anointed and gotten to bed. The process was repeated not only for three days but throughout the week while the odors of my cottage kept all but its occupants far afield. By Friday I was weary to the point of exhaustion, but the end was not yet. My small boy woke me in the middle of the night by crying out that something was biting him. I found his story all too true; and on Saturday morning we had a bonfire of his mattress and attacked his bed with corrosive sublimate and a feather. Few well-ordered boarding-schools today can afford three such plagues in one week or the requisite humor and endurance to combat them!

Throughout most of my life an indifferent sleeper, I slept at Hillside the sleep of the weary and the curiously contented. I became, in fact, so good at sleeping that when my twelve-year-old cried out on cold nights with the ear-ache, I could rise at once, heat a raisin on a hat-pin over my acetylene gas jet, stuff it in her ear with a bit of cotton to keep it there, and in the morning not feel entirely sure whether or not I had done it. This remedy, which my mother had used in my childhood and which I should recommend to all teachers were there nowadays any beneficent schools like Hillside, never failed to enable both me and the child to go back to sleep.

Saturday evening was always a pleasant time and occasion for the cottage teachers at Hillside, for then, after our charges were in bed, we met at one cottage or the other over our necessary mending. One week we patched trousers, sewed on buttons, and darned stockings for the small boys; the next we repaired rents, sewed on buttons and darned stockings for the smallest girls. The least efficient seamstress read aloud. These evenings were quiet enough in all conscience, and yet there was a sense of security about them which I like to remember.

The children at Hillside, both boys and girls, were responsible for the care of their rooms. My children were fined a penny for any article of clothing left about or for any toy out of place, and fines were ruthlessly collected each morning at eight o'clock when beds had been made and rooms tidied for the day. Saturday morning was a furious time of sweeping, beating rugs, and dusting, for all houses must be clean and orderly for Sunday before anyone could start for woods and fields.

6

No one who ever shared life at Hillside, teachers or children, will ever forget the Sundays there.

The Lloyd-Jones family was strongly Unitarian both in conviction and in splendid practice. In the preface to Jenkin Lloyd-Jones' *Diary* is the fol-

lowing entry: "The first Jenkin Jones preached
his first heretical sermon in his mother's garden
(in Wales) in 1726, ninety-three years before
Channing preached his Baltimore sermon (1819)
from which later event American Unitarianism
generally dates its beginning." The author of the
diary, who often visited Hillside and whom the
children greatly loved, was himself the third Jenkin to be a Unitarian minister.

In 1886 a small chapel had been built by the
family in a grove of pine trees at a cross-roads
a short distance from the school. On August 15th
of that year it was named Unity Chapel and dedicated to the memory of Richard and Mary Thomas
Lloyd-Jones. This chapel, brown and shingled,
plain, even austere without and within, was the
center and nucleus of the religious life at Hillside,
a life so normal and wholesome that everyone
there insensibly became a part of it. No other creed,
if creed it was, could have seemed so natural, indeed
so inevitable. One could enter "into the treasures
of the snow" and into the "sweet influences of the
Pleiades" at Hillside. One could "perceive the
breadth of the earth" and a "way for the lightning
and thunder" there simply because the sight and
sound of all things natural were made part and
parcel of our daily existence.

Everyone in the valley went to church on Sunday morning as a matter of course. So far as I
know there was no rule about it. Certain children

on Saturday afternoons took their turns at cleaning the chapel and decorating it with flowers in autumn and spring and with greens in winter for the Sunday morning service, and, with the exception of the few Catholic children, we all trooped there as a family at eleven o'clock.

We had no resident pastor, as the chapel had been built and dedicated only as a place of family worship. The aunts, the uncles, the teachers, sometimes one of the older boys or girls, sat in the pulpit, read the lesson, announced the hymns, read the prayers, gave a talk or read a sermon. Whether Uncle Enos, Aunt Nell, or Aunt Jennie was the preacher, or whether through them we heard the words of Theodore Parker, William Ellery Channing, William Gannett, or Ralph Waldo Emerson, the service was the same in its simplicity and reality. We were all there together in the silence of the fields without, covered with snow or springing into life; and I feel sure that God in His diverse and mysterious ways was never entirely absent even in the mind of the smallest and most uneasy child.

This same orderly and reverent spirit characterized our Sunday evening vespers in the schoolroom and our morning devotional exercises. This great common-room at school had been designed as much for a family gathering-place as for one of study. A huge fire-place was at one end, and on cold winter days logs were always burning. Upon the wide long stone above it was carved in Welsh, *The Truth against the world;* and around the brown timbers of the balcony which surrounded the room were cut into the wood these words from Isaiah: *They that wait upon the Lord shall renew their strength, they shall mount up with wings as eagles; they shall run and not be weary; they shall walk and not faint.* The boys and girls of high-school age sat about four huge oak tables, one for each class, and young children were each morning at the opening of school ranged in a long line on a bench at the side.

Our morning religious exercises were simple in the extreme and their simplicity was at once deepened and heightened by a custom or observance which I have never seen or known of elsewhere in any variety of schools. The aunts were ardent believers in the value of stillness, both of body and of mind, as a condition which might presumably hold rich gifts within itself. They would have contended that the truth in the miracle of the feeding of the five thousand lay not so much in the fact that everyone received bread and fish as in the command that everyone *sit down* in order to receive his portion. They did not, however, depend upon either precept or example of their own to develop a measure of self-discipline sufficient to enjoin the habit of occasional silence upon their teachers and children. Instead they ruthlessly imposed the habit upon us all for five days in the week.

When we were once assembled in the schoolroom, the small children on their bench, the boys and girls at their tables, the teachers in a long row of chairs facing the school, when the clock in the hall struck nine, complete stillness fell upon us all and lasted for exactly five minutes. During this time no one, not even the smallest, moved. Whether we thought of anything or of nothing during this period of silence was our own concern; but the slightest confusion on the part of any one of us merited and received stern reproof. In fact, the keeping of this silence for five long minutes and the relentless control of one's body even to one's toes and fingers was the one undeviating law of the Hillside Home School. When the five minutes were over, one of the aunts or teachers, or sometimes one of the older children, read from the Bible or from something else meet and proper. Then we said a prayer together and went at once to our respective rooms and tasks.

It is pleasant again to know in these days of mental and physical restlessness that some hundreds of us somewhere or other have kept still, even although we were made to do so, for certain accumulative hours of our lives. Even now in moments of silence that great, still room with its many motionless children comes into my mind and memory as perhaps the most abundant of all the abundance which Hillside held and gave so simply and unobtrusively to everyone within its encircling hills. There come, too, into my memory certain quick and confidential smiles exchanged on certain spring mornings between Aunt Jennie and a small boy on the long bench. He was named Dicky Cole, and he was a lover of birds. When the first meadow-lark sounded outside the casement windows, the sudden smile between them only deepened and made more reverent the silence.

7

Hillside was a school as well as a farm and a home. Indeed, it was the best school for children of all sorts and conditions that I have ever known. This was true largely, of course, because of the calibre of its teachers, and peculiarly true because its teachers had other responsibilities outside their class-rooms. Since their academic capital could never be divorced from the exigencies and necessities of normal living, the intellectual training which they gave their students was more vivid, alive, and real than it could have been under other circumstances. What boys and girls learned from their books at Hillside became inevitably related to the life which they lived and to the companionship which they enjoyed and trusted.

The two senior teachers in the school of my day

were two nieces of the aunts, daughters of Mary Lloyd-Jones, who in 1870 had married a Scotsman, James Philip by name. Uncle Philip, as we called him, had, too, a long white beard and keen, kind blue eyes. He lived on a near-by and beautiful farm a little above the valley; and his older daughter, known to us as Miss Elsie, who kept his home for him, came daily to the school to teach ancient history and mathematics. The younger daughter, Anna, whom we called Miss Nell, had charge of the small boys in West Cottage and taught French and German. Both were admirable teachers as well as delightful persons, and no young teacher could have had more tactful, friendly guidance than they gave to me. Their home, too, was always open to us; and I spent once a snowy Christmas there which I shall never forget. The former is now Mrs. John Lewis of Detroit; the latter, still a teacher, has taught for many years at St. Agnes School in Albany, New York.

The teacher of music, she who failed to detect the first of our three plagues in one week at Hillside, now admirably heads the department of music in the Francis Parker School in Chicago. The teacher of nature studies, to whom I owe more resources for pleasure than I can ever repay, is there likewise. The teacher of art now supervises that work in the public schools of Madison. The others, now with families of their own, have looked

in vain for a Hillside to supplement and complement their own responsibilities as parents.

The requirements made by the aunts of their
teachers in their class-rooms were strict and rigid;
but they were few in number. They insisted that
the life in studies be made as interesting and as
alive as the life outside them, in fact, inseparable
from it, that the play element within books seem
as natural as play itself. Like all good teachers
they saw no reason why any subject taught should
be unrelieved by curiosity on the part of the
teacher as well as on the part of the student. They
knew that learning is never dull, that only dull
teachers make it so. They knew that things in
books have meaning only as they are associated
with other things, either in books or outside them.
They cared nothing for methods as methods, were,
indeed, impatient with them, but they were avid
for results, which they saw in improved manners
and in an awakened sense of responsibility as well
as in grade sheets. They were so alive themselves
in all that they thought and did that they found it
difficult, if not impossible, to tolerate indifference
or half-heartedness on the part of their teachers.
Whatsoever our heads as well as our hands found
to do at Hillside, we did it with our might—or
we did not remain there.

Each child to both the aunts, whatever his age,
was a person rather than merely a child, with the
rights, privileges, and necessities of his own indi-

vidual make-up. Only one thing was expected of each: that he should live on decent terms with a large and decent family. Once he had learned to do this (and few had to learn) his talents, or want of them, were respected and his individual development in and out of school a matter of sane interest and concern to us all. If, indeed I could be sure that progressive education· today held and furthered the ideas and methods of Hillside, together with its lack of self-consciousness about them, I should mount the lecture platform on behalf of the "new" schools!

The college preparatory work at Hillside was a source of pride to the aunts. They followed their young men and women in the universities of the Middle West and in the eastern colleges and felt responsible for the intellectual capital which they carried with them wherever they went. They had no patience with work half done, and the very vigor of their natures made both teachers and students curiously ashamed of inattention and lack of self-discipline. They had a way of bursting into stormy Welsh to each other when some one of us had displeased them by laziness or lack of attention to detail; and the very fact that no one save themselves understood their vituperations rendered them all the more effective.

Both, indeed, had within themselves a strain of austerity. On occasion both could be severe, uncompromising, even pitiless. Aunt Jennie's righteous anger in particular was feared by teachers and children alike. When her black eyes flashed and her mouth tightened, the object of her indignation felt consumed with fire like the children of Israel before Jehovah. Yet the sources of her displeasure were so well known to us all that humiliation and shame seemed but just payment for thoughtlessness, neglect, or wrong-doing. Cruelty infuriated her. She could not brook in silence unkindness to animals or to children, or the persecution mental or physical of one child toward another, or of a teacher toward a child. Injustice, dishonesty, or unfairness were met with contempt and scorn as were laziness, irreverence, or vulgarity in any form. Yet I never knew her to be unreasonable or unfair in her dealings with any member of her large family, or to fail to be plunged into sorrow and contrition if her judgment had been hasty or her anger unmerited.

Few schools at any time or place have had headmistresses like Ellen and Jane Lloyd-Jones. It was impossible to live and to work with them and for their sane and splendid purposes without taking from them added vitality and enthusiasm. They were Hillside, and Hillside was they. Even the knowledge that anger could be released upon meet occasion created a wholesome fear in teachers and students alike of whatsoever things were unlovely, untrue, impure, and of bad report.

8

Aunt Jennie died in May, 1917, Aunt Nell two years later in November, 1919. They both lie in the family burying-ground behind the small brown chapel at the cross-roads. They had closed their school a few years before as there was seemingly no one to carry it on. I saw them for the last time in the winter of 1913 when the inroads of sickness and age, increased by certain family sorrows and anxieties, had begun to make themselves apparent. Yet it was impossible to think of them as old. And when twenty-five years later, in May two years ago, I went back to Hillside for the first time since 1913 and stood by their graves in the little church-yard, I could not think of them as dead. The former things had passed away, it was true; the school grounds and houses were untended and desolate; yet under the trees behind the chapel one felt as Matthew Arnold felt in Rugby Chapel about his father, another great teacher. Not, perhaps, that "somewhere surely afar" was still practised that strength of being, "zealous, beneficent, firm", but rather that zeal, beneficence, and strength had been created to life everlasting in the memories of us all once at Hillside by the two women who lay there.

Amiel says somewhere in his *Journal Intime* that in order truly to understand an experience one must not only completely live in it but come completely outside it as well. When I was young and first read these words, I was puzzled by them, as seemingly I could never completely separate myself from any experience which had meant anything at all to me. But now I know that to come completely outside some life-giving verity in human existence means simply the sifting of the mortal from the immortal, the corruptible from the incorruptible, in other words, the ability to preserve intact and curiously alive those things that cannot be shaken.

We travelled much in realms of gold at Hillside, saw many goodly sights of the earth, entered into many goodly kingdoms of the mind. We were watchers of the skies there. Whatever vision or imagination I have been able to give to my teaching in the years since then, I owe to two women in a Wisconsin valley thirty years ago; and I can only wish in all humility that any words of mine may prolong, if but for a season, their rightful immortality.

Chapter V

MRS. MOFFAT'S SCHOOL
FOR GIRLS

V

I SUPPOSE that a kind of uneasy ambition
prompted me to leave Hillside after three years
there. Surely it was nothing else. I wanted at
twenty-five to continue with my study. There was
an odd glamor surrounding advanced degrees in
those days before they had become as they are today an uneasy matter of course to all who are fit
for college teaching and to many who are not. The
future was still new and exciting to me, and I had
abundant health and strength for the untried fields
which I wanted to conquer. The fact that I had
no money for the conquering of them was a matter
of no consequence whatever. I would procure a
position in some large city which contained a university, I thought, and teach and study at the same
time.

Through the mother of one of my students at
Hillside I was put in touch with a certain girls'
school in Chicago, known as Mrs. Moffat's School;
and on a cold February day of my last year at
Hillside I journeyed thither to see its headmistress.

The result of my visit was precisely what I had hoped. I was asked to come to the school the following September to teach odds and ends for my room and board and five hundred dollars. At the same time I was promised the opportunity to begin my graduate work at the University of Chicago.

Although Mrs. Moffat's School for Girls, to give its complete title, is now no longer in existence, it will always exist in my mind and memory and stand me in good stead as a source of unquenchable humor and as a memorial of the days when literally nothing in the way of labor was able to daunt me. In 1912 and for the two years I remained within it the school was housed in a huge, rambling residence which had once been a house of some grandeur in the earlier days of Chicago. A spacious lawn surrounded it; a high hedge of lilacs protected it from at least a part of the dirt and noise of a certain dirty and noisy portion of the city. Within, the house was late Victorian in every sense, in its hushed, complacent atmosphere as well as in its furnishings. Even sixty lively girls from the best families of the neighborhood in 1912 could not banish the impression which it gave that it was decorously sure of itself and discreetly glad of it.

In contrast to the informality of Hillside, life at Mrs. Moffat's was formality itself. Seemliness and propriety were the order of the day. These guideposts also bounded and dominated our thinking if, indeed, the mental processes at Mrs. Moffat's School could, by a kind imagination, be termed thinking. The virtues which it strove to emboss upon the minds of its twelve boarding girls and some fifty day scholars were expressed by precept instead of suggested by example. One could reach out and touch these virtues, look at them, name them over and over. One knew them and yet did not know them, for they had an odd, external, even extraneous quality and seemed always to be outside one instead of inside.

The promoter of these virtues, and, it is only fair to say, the possessor of them, was the headmistress, Mrs. Abbie Moffat, who at my time of entrance into the school was in her early seventies. I never understood Mrs. Moffat at close range, but in retrospect I can easily see that she was the best possible example of her upbringing and background. Her father had been a Presbyterian clergyman in the Middle West somewhere, a man who, according to Mrs. Moffat, "saw his duty simply and clearly and did it." Mrs. Moffat was also one of the last of a certain type of headmistress not uncommon to the nineteenth century, but in the twentieth practically extinct in any sort of school. She was distinctly of and for an age, not, fortunately, for all time; and yet no given age can claim a copyright on its Mrs. Moffats. She admirably fulfilled the injunction of St. Paul that we should be *doers* of the Word and not hearers only—an injunction, I confess, which has always irritated me. Mrs. Moffat, in fact, was too engrossed in perpetual doing—for her girls, for her especial district of Chicago and its various institutions, and for what she termed "progress in general"—for her to take a moment to *hear* anything whatsoever. Justification by good works was her watchword, and she admirably exemplified and fulfilled it.

One was never uncomfortably conscious of the insistence upon moral values at Hillside. The very fact that they were seldom talked about lent proof to their presence. They were simply taken for granted. At Mrs. Moffat's they were never allowed to remain invisible or even intangible, and no one of them was ever taken for granted. Mrs. Moffat lined up the moral values each year on dress parade and presented them to us. They became ours whether we wanted them or not merely by the rigor of her imposition.

The first, indeed the all-inclusive, moral value to Mrs. Moffat was *duty,* duty to her, to the school, to Chicago, and to "progress in general". Whenever we had visitors at our morning exercises in the school parlors, she always told them and retold us that the one aspiration and favorite word of the school was *duty*. When she had said this, we always, in proof of her contention, sang the school song, which she many years before had chosen *as* the school song. It ran in these words to a most sentimental tune:

Who treads the path of duty
Nor shrinks when honor calls,
Fills life with noble beauty,
And ne'er inglorious falls.

For two years I heard duty so emulated as a virtue and so harped on as a word that years ago I cast it from my vocabulary as a spurious term and, I fear, so far as possible from my character as a much over-rated asset to worth in general. Could the virtue itself only have been accorded another name from the many that describe it so much more graciously, I, for one, should have lived on better terms with it at Mrs. Moffat's.

Yet I doubt if any other name could have been accurately used to describe the special variety of duty which fired Mrs. Moffat and which she strove to re-kindle daily in us. Duty to her was not, for example, what it was to Wordsworth. To be sure, it might be a rod to check the erring; or even a stern lawgiver; but assuredly it wore no benignant grace. No flowers laughed before it; no fragrance trod in its footing. Nor had it any relationship whatever with the stars or the most ancient heavens. Mrs. Moffat's duty was quite unrelieved by philosophy and an entire stranger to meditation. It was, instead, the urge which kept her going eighteen hours out of every twenty-four and which she imposed on all of us to keep us going also.

It is only fair to grant, however, that Mrs. Mof-

fat's duty had brought forth and maintained a
well-run school, good, if pedantic, teaching both
by herself and others, and any number of deeds of
mercy done to any number of persons outside our
lilac hedge as well as within it. Doubtless, without this driving sense of duty, so much more in-
grained in the last century than now, she would
never have accomplished all the things which she
had brought to really splendid fruition in her long
life. Left a widow with several small children at
a relatively early age, she had brought up and
educated her large family without the least sense
of persecution by fate or of inability to realize her
aim. She had opened a small school in her home
in a neighboring city while her children were still
young; and the school in Chicago, which her success as a teacher had made possible, had been for
several years the fulfillment of her early desire
and necessity. Perhaps the strict Presbyterianism
in which she had been reared had more than a
little to do with her fervid, if obvious, carrying
out of any number of gospel precepts.

Mrs. Moffat was an imposing if not a subtle
woman. What she had missed in delicacy of perception she made up for by diligence in business.
According to King Solomon she should have stood
before all the kings of all the earth; and I can
think of no one who would have so enjoyed it. She
was literally never idle; and it was a source of
curiosity to me to note how her fundamentally unim-

aginative mind was forever conjuring up new and necessary duties to be performed. She had broken a leg some years before my arrival at the school, but this infirmity impaired her not at all. She could use her crutch equally well to walk with, to evince displeasure, or to point at any visible disorder or confusion which needed to be set to rights at once.

She was, in her way, a fine-looking woman. Refusing stolidly to yield in any way to current fashions, she did her gray hair high with a tortoise shell comb to keep it in place and with a meticulously arranged curl on either cheek. She always wore black satin; indeed, through two years I never remember seeing her in anything else. She was very large and short, and she wore long, full skirts, with a modified basque above them relieved at the neck with a bit of white lace and a gold brooch. Except for the morning exercises, for which she came downstairs, and for her meals, which she never missed, she ruled her school from her upstairs sitting-room. At morning exercises, when the school was assembled in the front parlors, she descended the stairs on her crutch quite without help, crossed the room with great dignity, cleared her throat, for she was afflicted by laryngitis, and said,

"Good morning, girls."
Upon which girls and teachers alike rose and called back,

"Good morning, Mrs. Moffat."

She always listened carefully to this rejoinder, for she was fond of quoting from *King Lear* how excellent in woman is a soft and low voice; and if she detected any stridency in any voice out of the seventy in the room, she always spoke of it in private to the offender.

Mrs. Moffat's avowed purpose, even in 1912, was to rear and train "Christian gentlewomen". This term to her expressed not only all the necessary virtues but all the socially acceptable ones as well. She was not overly concerned as to the intellectual and academic attainments of her students; but she was eager that they should in good time establish decent homes and feel a responsibility toward society and toward "progress in general". Since she did not know how to accomplish this quite honest aim and desire except by precept upon precept, and since she had sprung from an age and environment in which there were less irritation and no humor in the constant piling up of precepts, precepts were her stock in trade. She encouraged the admission to her school of the rich because she felt and said (not without truth) that the rich were needier than the poor. They had greater responsibilities, she said, to render unto the Dispenser of all good gifts. She was determined that no recipient of monetary talents in her school should bury them in a napkin or hide them in a field. And her many ways of avoiding this catastrophe were planned to give credit not only to the generous and financially able among us, but to the school as well.

We were frequently told at morning exercises that a day begun without a cheery smile or a helpful word to those less fortunate than we was a day lost both to ourselves and to our Maker. The questionable logic of this statement was obscured by its constant repetition. We were forever dispensing gifts to the poor, forever being commanded to count our blessings as we noted how "the other half" lived. We knew and visited orphan asylums to bear cheer and encouragement to those within. There was a home for old ladies directly opposite the school, a place seemingly bestowed upon us by Providence, Mrs. Moffat said, in order that we be spared the awful consequences of self-satisfaction and selfishness.

Mrs. Moffat never turned her broad back upon any demands of Providence even although she herself invented them; and this old ladies' home gave her scope and material for one of her characteristic innovations. She decided early in my first year that not only cheer in life might be brought by the school to certain of the aged women there but compensation in death as well. This compensation, as she conceived it, was the burial of certain of the aged, who had no close relatives, from the school parlor. Mrs. Moffat went at funerals in the same fervor with which she attacked all other occasional events, especially if they were the fruit of her own mind; and she early enlisted me as her assistant.

I do not remember how many funerals we staged in the front parlor of the school. Perhaps the details of all were carried out with such rigid similarity, such undeviating precision, that I cannot now distinguish one funeral from another. The order of events was always the same. Since the day scholars were free at one o'clock and lunch was over by two, funerals were usually set for two-thirty. At two we got ready for the undertaker, to whom Mrs. Moffat unwillingly relinquished certain preliminaries and finalities which seemed, even to her, unquestionably his own. Getting ready for the funeral meant arranging the chairs in the parlor, placing flowers which had been extorted from divers patrons and friends of the school, and getting ourselves appropriately dressed. It also meant the winding of Mrs. Moffat's crutch with yards of black crape and tying the ends in a wide and long bow at the cross-piece. I became an expert at this odd ceremony, which she always supervised with the greatest care.

I was the only teacher actually required to attend the funerals although others often came. I think they felt a bit uneasy over neglecting what Mrs. Moffat termed an opportunity for quiet reflection and deeper thought. My presence was required partly because Mrs. Moffat needed an assistant, partly because, according to her, I looked young, healthy, and cheerful. She and I always descended the stairs arm in arm, when the proper moment came, but we never entered the parlor until all were assembled before the coffin of the old lady who was being compensated.

Infrequently some of the girls who were resident in the house sang a hymn, but usually not, as Mrs. Moffat was never quite able to gauge the possible effect upon them of this unusual occasion. They were instead commanded to remain in respectful silence in their rooms upstairs; and we sensibly collected our music from other and sometimes odd quarters. Some minister read the scripture, which Mrs. Moffat had selected for him, but, after he had learned from her any helpful items about the deceased, he was left to his own devices in the matter of prayer.

The dramatic moment always came at the close of the procedure, for then Mrs. Moffat read a poem which she had written. This was either a votive poem on the accomplishments of the dead, if she had had obvious accomplishments, or a poem of general reflection on the nature of the occasion. I always carried the poem in the pocket of my blue suit, which Mrs. Moffat had chosen as the most appropriate of my clothing, and gave it to her after I had helped her to her feet and walked with her to the head of the coffin.

Mrs. Moffat was a poet of no mean ability even

in poems of the graveyard school. She had a real feeling for words, discrimination in their use, and a fine sense of rhythm. Yet upon occasion her feeling for both rhyme and rhythm deserted her. An illustration of this sudden desertion occurred one afternoon when we were compensating a certain old lady whose Christian name was Carlotta. Carlotta had been a woman of parts in her day, and Mrs. Moffat's rather long poem recounted these in ballad form. Unfortunately, at intervals between the stanzas Mrs. Moffat had been impelled to insert a refrain, the poignant emotion of which was obscured by her quite obvious difficulty in procuring suitable rhyme. This refrain ran:

> Farewell to Carlotta
> Her life is our motto.

Although Mrs. Moffat's humor could not be depended upon (for she never saw the slightest thing funny about the funerals) she had, paradoxically enough, a fine wit. She loved plays on words, was extraordinarily good at puns, and was, in short, no mean neologist when opportunity arose.

2

My position in Mrs. Moffat's school was somewhat anomalous. In teaching I was responsible for the odds and ends which no one else wanted or had time to do. Among my subjects were nature study, beginning algebra, German, geography, civics, and English grammar. My class-room was in the cellar beyond the furnace-room, which situation really lacked the grimness of its connotation as it was a large, bright room with many high windows. When I had once reached it, I always felt like a shade released from the pit of Acheron into the Elysian Fields.

Most of my classes were made up of young children of thirteen or thereabouts whom I greatly enjoyed. They were, for the most part, well-bred youngsters with good manners if with no great love of learning. We grew plants in my room and kept a somewhat desolate aquarium in an old sink. The teaching was easy enough, which was fortunate as I had small time to prepare my lessons; and the mental agility it required of me in skipping from one subject to another was not without its value.

With the exception of one teacher in the early forties, whom now I should call young but who at the time seemed far removed from me, I was the only young teacher in the school. The others were of late middle age, and, adequate even efficient as I believe they were as teachers, meant little to me as persons. Practically all of them lived elsewhere than in the school, and I saw little of them.

As a matter of rather stern fact, my real job in Mrs. Moffat's school was not that of a teacher at all. I was instead private secretary, lady's maid, and attendant in general upon Mrs. Moffat. This post had its compensations, for she was never without interest to me at any hour of the day or night or in the discharging of any duties which her fertile mind could conceive. My reasonable skill at typewriting, which I had taught myself, proved of great service to her, for she was the most prolific and versatile of letter-writers.

She dictated dozens of letters each week, which I pounded out on a somewhat decrepit machine in her sitting-room. I enjoyed this occupation vastly for, although I learned soon to guess the probable contents of our letters, I was sure to be taken aback by the address.

We might, and did, write to President Wilson to tell him of our Presbyterianism and to rejoice in his; or to Mr. John Galsworthy to tell him that the school had greatly profited by certain of his sketches; or to a prominent soap company to say that, much as we liked most of their products, we detected a somewhat vulgar scent in a certain soap and deplored its manufacture as below their standard of excellence. We wrote to statesmen, mayors, clergymen, and rabbis; financiers, actors, college presidents, and physicians; columnists, cartoonists, and wardens of prisons. We wrote to Mr. A. E. Housman to thank him for his poem on the cherry tree and to tell him that we recited this poem in chorus every spring. We wrote to Mr. H. G. Wells to take exception to certain of his educational ideas and to put certain pertinent questions to him. When Mr. Wells had neglected for some months to answer our letter, we wrote him again. We wrote to Mr. Thomas Hardy to suggest a somewhat brighter point of view toward the universe, reminding him that, in our opinion, one held one's fate in one's own strong hands, and acknowledging that we should like his characters immeasurably better if they had more spirit in them to struggle on. Mrs. Alice Meynell, whose poems were in those days attracting attention, received word from us that, although we could not follow her religious thinking, we were grateful for her poem on thoughts as flocks of sheep, since we could use it in our character building at school. Our letters were thus admonitory, appreciative, advisory as occasion demanded.

This indomitable urge toward letter writing usually attacked Mrs. Moffat late at night. She had a gong fixed at the entrance to the third floor where I had my room; and when this gong sounded at any time between ten and midnight, I descended at once to her sitting-room, and we began to draw the far-flung world of art, industry, social betterment and learning closer about us. Mrs. Moffat always contended that she did not need to sleep. She could not bear, she said, now that conceivably her days might be numbered, to lose any opportunity for a larger life.

Between our letters Mrs. Moffat talked. I have
never since then read Lytton Strachey's study of
Lady Hester Stanhope without being reminded of
Mrs. Moffat. For Mrs. Moffat's talk like Lady
Hester's jumped all barriers and encircled the
world. New England "Brahminism" was one of
her topics which she loved; Tristan da Cunha was
another, although just why that most lonely out-
post of the Atlantic should consume a person like
her with excitement I could never understand.
Browning, then in greater vogue than now, was a
third; W. E. Henley was a fourth. She dearly
loved to quote *Rabbi Ben Ezra,* to encourage me
to grow old along with her, which I was rapidly
doing under her constant surveillance. She could
never decide whether she preferred the *Epilogue
to Asolando* or *Invictus,* whether never to turn
one's back but to march breast forward actually
meant more than to be master of one's fate and cap-
tain of one's soul out of the dark that covered one.

Not that Mrs. Moffat was covered by any discernible mental or spiritual darkness. She was
rather sitting most safely in a most comfortable
chair while her thoughts and words ranged over
the stern (if distant) realities of life. We always
had a luncheon at midnight. Mrs. Moffat sent me
to her adjoining bedroom where a servant had
earlier placed ham sandwiches, apple pie, and
milk. We fared sumptuously while she talked on,
or sometimes came down to earth to consider the

next charitable move the school should encourage in order to make itself really felt in Chicago.

Mrs. Moffat had an irritating way of never recognizing anything which she did not wish to recognize. She never recognized, for instance, the presence of rats on the third floor in spite of our voluble terror of them. They were simply not there to her. She never recognized that certain of her girls were mentally unable to pass their subjects, or that other schools in Chicago were better in every respect than her own, or that the housekeeper was old and inefficient, or that replies to most of her letters were not forthcoming. She had constructed her world precisely as she wanted it, and she sat within it, benign, contented, benevolent, and completely sure of herself.

3

I am convinced that Mrs. Moffat was quite unconscious of failing in her promise to me of graduate work at the University of Chicago. Indeed, she took pleasure in telling any number of persons that her youngest teacher was working toward a doctor's degree at the University. Graduate work was one of those outside interests which she was always encouraging because she could not bear, she said, that her teachers should not be alive to glorious opportunities for the making of a new world. Studying, however, except the necessary modicum of it, was rarely done at Mrs. Moffat's. We were always so up and doing there, always so achieving or pursuing with hearts for any fate, that we quite naturally had small time for study.

My fate at Mrs. Moffat's was to learn to labor unceasingly and, while laboring, to wait as patiently as possible for a rare half hour over my books. I registered for two seminars at Chicago, one in philosophy, the other in history, and attended them when I was not shopping for Mrs. Moffat, or calling on the sick and aged, or managing a funeral, or writing letters, or taking unwilling girls to the Art Institute, or sleeping the sleep of the exhausted on the third floor.

My professor of philosophy was a little man, Professor Talbert by name, who lived outside this world as completely as Mrs. Moffat lived within it, or at least within her version of it. If he remembers me at all, which is unlikely, he remembers me as a poorly prepared and often sleepy student. But I remember him and am grateful to him because he apparently could and did live in his world without so much as a notion of what Mrs. Moffat's was like. He conducted his seminar on the subject of mysticism; and I shall always be in debt to him partly for certain books to which he introduced me, mostly for his eyes which were an outward and visible proof of what the books tried to say. One of these books was William James' *The Varieties of Religious Experience,* an-

other Rudolf Eucken's *The Life of the Spirit.*
Even although I was in a perpetual state of irritation at Mrs. Moffat's, I was always able to see the humor in trying to comprehend and to appreciate mystical states under her roof. If humor resides in a rigidity of consciousness, as Bergson states in his essay, or, in other words, in the sudden collision of two worlds, Mrs. Moffat's School for Girls certainly afforded any number of excellent examples of that collision. Whatever else life was there, it was funny in the extreme. I have often since wondered whether Mrs. Moffat's world collided in any appreciable sense when she left it with the one which awaited her and over the framing of which she had had no control. I should hate to think that all her careful preparations, all her weighing and measuring for whatever Judgment Day awaited her, have all been for naught. She always hated to be taken unawares, and surprises of any nature were distasteful to her. Just as she knew precisely what she wanted in this world, the prices to be paid, the rewards which followed good deeds, so she knew precisely what she expected of the next. And if that next world is run, not on a system of rewards and punishments, of ways and means, causes and consequences, but rather along the lines of Professor Talbert's sense of Reality, Mrs. Moffat must be sadly out of her element there.

She once observed to me in a rare moment of

interest in my precarious graduate work that the moral and social aspects of philosophy chiefly concerned her. Man's duty to his fellowman, she said, engaged all her time and energy; and personally she felt, with all due respect for the mystics, that they had contributed little of downright and tangible value to life, nothing, in fact, that one could seize upon for real inspiration while one strove to be of use to one's day and generation. She concluded her observations by deploring that one so young as I, one on the threshold of achievement as it were, should be seemingly so interested in the intangible and invisible. She thought that hard, definite work would afford the best possible antidote to any "flighty" tendency I might possess; and she assured me that she would duly see that my feet were securely anchored to the ground. This promise Mrs. Moffat was amply able to keep, and she kept it.

BERLIN AND BLANKENBURG

VI

I WENT to Europe for the first time in the spring of 1913. I went primarily to study German, a language in which I had been deeply interested for one year in college and which I was attempting to teach at Mrs. Moffat's school. No one but myself knew how badly I was teaching it; even Mrs. Moffat characteristically refused to recognize that I was in no way fit to do so; but when I asked to be allowed to leave school three weeks before its close in order to have a longer summer in Europe, Mrs. Moffat generously said that she considered it her duty and in the interest of her school to procure a substitute for my work at her own expense.

I might with equal advantage to myself, so far as a sufficient mastery of German grammar for teaching it was concerned, have studied in any one of a number of reputable summer schools; yet such a course of study seemed uninteresting to me. I had dreamed of foreign travel ever since I had listened to my grandmother and her friends at home; my ancestors had not sailed the seas without bequeathing a similar urge to me; and this honest necessity for learning more of a language which I was trying to teach afforded me a valid reason for such an unprecedented step. My father, who would have considered improvident and senseless the spending of my total savings to date merely on European travel, was not indisposed toward spending them on further study.

In 1913 the sum of five hundred dollars for three months in Europe was not only adequate but generous. One's berth on a cabin liner or second-class on a three-class ship cost from fifty to seventy-five dollars. My return fare on the White Star steamship *Teutonic,* now no more, was exactly one hundred and eighteen dollars and fifty cents. With a lesson each day from a teacher in Berlin at three marks an hour I still possessed an intoxicating amount of capital, which my father enjoined me to handle with care but which I determined in secret to spend as recklessly as I liked.

My students today who slip down Ambrose Channel by the hundreds once college is over in June can have no conception of what going to Europe for the first time meant in 1913 to a young teacher of twenty-six who had earned the money for it all herself. So engrossing was that journey for months in prospect, so satisfying in actuality, and so enchanting in retrospect that no aspect of it—the ship and her furnishings, the people at my

table, their faces, even their names, the interior
of my cabin, the sea at all hours, the things to eat
—has faded from my memory. Indeed, these things
have never once been touched by the dimness of
memory, never once threatened by its uncertainty.
When I look upon them now, I have the odd sen-
sation that they are not within the province of
things remembered, but that rather, because of
the intense reality they held for me, they have
been projected from the past to live by my side
in the present.

It was the same with all other aspects and hap-
penings of that extraordinary summer. All the
events and situations, all the places and persons,
all the weathers of many days—a chaffinch in a
Warwickshire garden, a sky-lark in a Surrey field,
the light through the arches of a cloister in Mi-
chaelstein, a child crying by a fountain in a Berlin *platz,* a cake in a *conditorei* in Charlottenburg
with tiny fir trees shining with icing, a little man
in a third-class carriage from Mainz to Berlin eat-
ing violet-scented candies at precisely four o'clock
in the afternoon—these things and hundreds like
them, I am convinced, are, by some odd process of
perpetual re-creating, in my present rather than in
my past.

Doubtless because of this curious re-creating
quality common to all things of that summer, my
two German teachers spring into new life whenever my attention is recalled to them. There they

are, not in my past but in my present, one in her sitting-room in Charlottenburg, the other in her stone-flagged dining-room in a Harz mountain town; one terrifying me to resentful tears, the other making me oddly conscious of a permanent, underlying sadness in the most pleasant of pastimes.

Fräulein Franke had become my somewhat bitter portion through the kind recommendation of my German professor at college, who had once borne and greatly profited by her mad ministrations. When after a fortnight in England I reached Berlin in mid-June, I called upon Fräulein Franke at once in response to a summons from her.

I found her that day as I was to find her every day for six weeks in her sitting-room of an upstairs apartment in Charlottenburg. She wore as she was to wear every day for six weeks a black stuff skirt, a white shirtwaist, and a red knitted jacket which, I found, she was constantly ravelling, but which was always whole the next day like a hundred things in the fairy tales. She was sitting, when I was ushered into her presence by an austere maid, next a great, towering stove, which completely filled a corner of the room from floor to ceiling. She had her feet on a foot-stool, and she seemed to be studying the stove, which was surely worth the time and effort since practically every tile in it was of differing color and design.

She rose and greeted me, not unkindly and yet without the slightest kindness. My poor, halting sentences became at once both the source of her displeasure and the reason for her continued existence. During our first interview she spoke the first, last, and only words of English I ever heard her speak to me or to anyone else, although she had a decent command of that language and might often have helped me on my way thereby. I think she was afraid that I should not get in German the inexorableness of her question, that I should not understand what manner of woman she was. Only because of these fears, I know, did she descend to English.

"You work?" she said. "I trouble with no one who does not work. You understand me? You understand me well?"

I assured her that work was precisely the reason that I had come to Berlin. Yet had I known her meaning of that simple verb, I should then and there have fled her awful presence as the scriptural children fled from the presence of the Elisha bears.

We began immediately to enter upon that work, and for six weeks we continued therein. I rose every morning at six to work for four hours as I had never worked before; at three I sat down again to work; at eight I settled myself to work until midnight. Only from five until seven in the late afternoon did I dare to leave the books she had made me buy to walk the Berlin streets in a hopeless attempt to forget her, waiting for me at eleven every day by her great stove.

Fräulein Franke's methods were ruthless, Prussian, Bismarckian. She gave me every morning one hundred small slips of paper encircled neatly with a rubber band, for my pocket. On each slip was a German expression, or idiom, with its English equivalent. These were to form the intolerable burden of our conversation for half an hour the next day at eleven o'clock. She gave me fifty sentences in English to be put into proper German. She gave me a fairy tale, the substance of which I was to recite to her the next day. She gave me a play of Schiller, one scene of which each day I was to criticise thoughtfully in good German.

Fräulein Franke's ruthless methods were supplemented by ruthless behavior. She knew neither mercy nor patience. She screamed at mistakes. *"Gott im Himmel, muss ich dieses Deutsch ertragen? Ich kann nicht! Ich will nicht!"* (God in Heaven, must I endure this German? I cannot! I will not!) Her screams were sufficiently humiliating in all conscience, but she never stopped at screaming. She had a heavy, three-cornered yellow pencil, the like of which I have never seen elsewhere, and this she used to good, if painful, advantage as her quick eyes ran the length of my

exercise sheets upon which I had written my fifty
sentences. The least of errors brought down the
yellow pencil upon the knuckles of my hand nearer
her. My association with Fräulein Franke became
after a few days more a game than anything else.
I was playing it for a stake: namely, that I should
never be brought to tears before her. I wept copi-
ously as I walked the two miles from the *pension*
in Motzstrasse where I lived to Charlottenburg
between ten and eleven, mumbling over my German idioms. I wept always on my way home. My
eyes were constantly swollen during my six weeks
in Berlin. It is no wonder that I always see that
hard and brittle city through a strange, unfamiliar
haze. But I won my game, for I never wept in
her presence either from her screams or from the
yellow pencil.

When I had finished my lesson at noon, I descended Fräulein Franke's stairs to the street and
did her shopping for her. This was a part of my
lesson, and Fräulein Franke always made me feel
that she was sacrificing a great pleasure in not
doing it herself. I bought fresh eggs, *frische Eier,
die besten,* rolls of sausage, loaves of bread, a new
broom, a bucket, *kuchen,* and fruit. Once I bought
her a chemise after a mortifying experience in a
man-run shop. When I brought my packages back,
she opened them at once in my trembling presence to ascertain whether they corresponded with

the list which she had given me in German. If they pleased her, she swept the lot with a withering gesture across the table upon which I had placed them; if they did not, she screamed at me.

Fräulein Franke had other students, but since unlike me they had no game at stake, they faded out one by one, and she watched them go with a fine scorn. Among them were two English boys of sixteen or thereabouts whom she had with misgivings consented to teach. They weathered her but a week; or perhaps it would be more accurate to say that she endured them. They always were dismissed at exactly eleven so that I invariably met them emerging as I was entering. We used to exchange fleeting, pregnant glances at her door, aware that she awaited her next victim at the top of her stairs.

She terminated her unwelcome acquaintance with them in a characteristic manner. For on the morning of their departure they both came hurtling down the stairs like so much luggage and into the street as I opened the door. When they had picked themselves up, they paused long enough to beg me not to go for my lesson. She was worse than ever, they said. She had literally thrown them from her room and down the stairs without so much as waiting for the thirty marks they owed her.

When I ascended the stairs, I found her laughing for the first and only time in my association with her. She was, in fact, shaking with mirth by the great tiled stove. *"Engländer werden sich niemals richtig benehmen,"* she said. *"Lass sie gehen —sofort. Ich mag sie nicht!"* (The English cannot be disciplined. They will not work. Let them go—let them go at once. I do not like them!)

My New England accent infuriated Fräulein Franke. In that respect I was almost as bad as the English, she said. She knew I *could* put *r's* in the right places if I only would; but since I clearly would not, she could never be sure whether I knew my cases or not. Together with my irritating accent, which she said was *furchtbar, schrecklich, scheusslich!* (astounding, horrible, ugly!) she suspected that I had no ear for music, which on one embarrassing morning she proved to her horror by making me sing at her organ. Americans, she said, were her worst students. They had no music in them, which meant that they had no feelings. This announcement she illustrated by beating her starched shirtwaist violently beneath her red jacket.

Yet, stormy as were our sessions, I think she rather liked me. Perhaps she was forced to do so simply because of my dogged tenacity. At all events when August came on and I was about to leave her for gentler treatment in the Harz, she invited me to spend the winter by the great stove in her house. To this overwhelming invitation I could find no suitable German gratitude and thanked her in English, which brought upon me a frightful burst of anger. My instinctive return to my own language, she said, proved that I had, as she had long suspected, no feelings whatsoever.

2

I was not sorry to leave Berlin nor have I ever had the least desire to return to it. Unlike the cities of the south, which I was to know in later years, unlike even Hamburg with its lively red and white sailed boats on the blue water of Elbe, it seemed to me a friendless place, hard, indifferent, and unyielding like the battalions of gray soldiers forever marching down Unter den Linden. It seemed to me that I could never penetrate beneath its clean, callous, benumbed exterior to feel even in a measure at home. Perhaps this impression emanated not from the city itself but only from Fräulein Franke's sitting-room in Charlottenburg. But wherever it came from, I was glad to leave its neat *plätze* with their orderly flowers, its immaculate streets, and its white-clad policemen who seemed to be watching even me, in tears, as I walked to and from my lesson.

Fräulein Franke, in spite of her screams and the sharp, painful raps of her yellow pencil, had written in my behalf to Fräulein Elise Elster of Blankenburg-am-Harz; and thither I journeyed early in August to continue my elusive pursuit of the German tongue. I can never forget my entrance into *das Elsterhaus* on a bright August afternoon or my welcome there.

The house itself is always present with me, not as a memory so much as a permanent and irremovable possession which I would never be without. It was a large house near the summit of a high hill, on the right side of a narrow cobbled street of bright plastered houses. When I had alighted from the cab and stood before it with Fräulein Elster, who had met me at the station, I thought it uninteresting enough although I liked its bright pink color. But when the door had opened and we passed at once through a flagged passage-way into the garden at the back, I thought and still think it the most enchanting of houses.

Perhaps, indeed, the back of *das Elsterhaus* was its front. For above the garden its pink walls were brighter than those above the street, and the pinkness was made further impressive by the addition of bright purple shutters which flanked all the windows. The garden of this unique and lovely house at once supplemented and completed its color scheme; for the long beds and borders reaching to the summer house at its end were brilliant with pink geraniums and verbenas and purple heliotrope. The sun lay warm on the garden after a shower earlier in the afternoon, and the fragrance of the heliotrope was everywhere.

Once I had been shown to my room above the

garden and had discovered that the smell of the
heliotrope was there also, we had coffee and cakes
in the summer house. I almost shattered the tran-
quil atmosphere of this kind occasion by the
springing of tears to my eyes when Fräulein Elster praised my German. I had forgotten in the
rigor of the past weeks that there was such a
pleasant thing as praise still abroad in the world;
and Fräulein Elster's generous words suddenly attacked my throat, making it difficult for me to
swallow my piece of currant cake.

I stayed three weeks at *das Elsterhaus*. Here
Germany was Germany as we like best to remember and know it. The household consisted, besides
Fräulein Elster, of two equally gracious women,
Fräulein Sonnamann, who taught English in a
Blankenburg school, and Fräulein Trobitsius, who
managed the house and fashioned wondrous three-
tiered cakes with fairy tales running up their sides
and terminating in a dramatic incident upon the
top. Fräulein Sonnamann was tall and handsome;
Fräulein Trobitsius short and fat; Fräulein Elster
small and lively with oddly sad eyes and crinkly
fair hair, which was always escaping from a tight
knot on the top of her head. They all laughed a
great deal and sent forth such an atmosphere of
good humor, contentment, and hospitality that I
wondered what queer, weak place in Fräulein
Franke's Prussian armor had ever induced her to
send me here.

In addition to the household proper there was an old, unattached man whose name I have forgotten if I ever knew it. He never came to meals; where he slept was a mystery; but he was always at the end of the garden where he watched, tended, and wrote about a colony of ants there. He seemed to live with, in, and because of *die Ameisen,* and I found him a great source of interest and pleasure. He was a tall, elderly man with short, bristling white mustachios. He had lost an arm in the Franco-Prussian War.

Besides me there were four other students: a professor of English at Williams College, an American girl of seventeen, a young master from Hotchkiss School, and an odd English woman of middle age, who was, if possible, more stupid at German than I. Ill-assorted though we might have been under ordinary circumstances, we became a family over night in the genial atmosphere all about; and although I now know of the whereabouts and destiny of only one of my companions, I still feel as though they belong to my life in a peculiar sense.

Our days at *das Elsterhaus* were so similar in their hours and minutes that it seems odd to look upon them as separate entities and realities. Yet each was filled and surrounded by so much brightness and pleasure, each was so complete in itself, that each stands separately as a value unto itself instead of merging with all the others.

We had breakfast at eight in a stone-flagged dining-room which looked out upon the garden. We sat at a polished table of some light-colored wood which caught the sun. There was always a glass jar of strained honey in the center which held the sun also and which has since become a kind of Platonic *universal* of all honey to me. Since there was no terror at *das Elsterhaus,* the conversation, if not fluent, was always easy and pleasant. After breakfast Fräulein Elster gave us each a half hour of German in the garden until we had a *zweite Frühstück* of rye bread, cold sausage, and beer at eleven o'clock. We had a substantial lunch at one, after which we went for a long walk through the black hills of the Harz.

Fräulein Elster was a fine walker. She carried a long alpenstock, more to point or gesticulate with than as a help in walking. I have rarely seen so much life in any human frame as in Fräulein Elster's almost diminutive one. She loved Germany with a passion and thought her own portion of it the most desirable and perfect of homes. She was a storehouse of stories about the Harz and was forever calling us together so that she might tell them to us with sudden and appropriate wavings and stampings of her alpenstock. She always had a goal for every walk: a fine tree somewhere, the view from a certain fir-clad summit, a waterfall, the ruins of a robber baron's stronghold, a splendid sweep of purpling heather. We always stopped somewhere for coffee at five o'clock. Fräulein Elster would allow us no *kuchen,* however, but that of Fräulein Trobitsius which she carried with her in a stout straw basket.

Of all times of the day, evenings at *das Elsterhaus* were the best. There was often some guest for supper so that we might have not only added practice in speaking but also an opportunity to meet other German people. These guests were usually men and usually teachers in some local school or in the *gymnasium.* As I remember them, they all had smooth, florid faces, rather formal manners, and stiff mustachios. We talked often at supper on current questions of the day; and I remember especially the discomfiture of Miss Sherborn, the English woman, when she tried in vain to vent her rage in German against the Welsh Church Disestablishment Bill.

After supper we followed an unvaried program which nightly repetition made only more enchanting. The table was cleared while we had coffee in the garden, and, when we reappeared, had been covered with a red and white checked cloth. Fräulein Elster then took her place at the head with a volume of Hans Andersen, and we all sat about her. She always read Hans Andersen to us instead of the Grimm brothers, Danish though he was. We had no other book for reading aloud while I was at *das Elsterhaus.* I do not think he was chosen merely because of the easy German of stories already familiar to us, but instead because Fräulein Elster so loved him.

"Er ist ein grosser Philosoph," she would say when she had finished *The Tin Soldier* or *The Little Match Girl*. *"Er ist ein weiser Mann. Er ist kein müssiger Erzähler von Kindergeschichten."*

("He is a great philosopher. He is a wise man. He is no idle teller of tales for children.")

Much of his wisdom crept into her voice in the quiet room, and all of his charm.

When the reading was over, we sang hymns and songs in a little parlor off the dining-room, standing around a small and wheezy organ. I always thought, as one or another of the Germans present made their selection of songs, how odd it was that they invariably selected those sad or with an undercurrent of sadness. "They amused themselves sadly after the fashion of their country," Hazlitt quotes Froissart as saying of the English. This was doubly true of the Germans at *das Elsterhaus*. All the songs and hymns they chose had in them, in their words or music, and often in both, the *sunt lacrimae rerum* of life from its beginning.

Fräulein Elster, I thought, was most truly herself at these singings. She sat at the organ, never looking at the music before her, her voice echoing pleasantly all the sorrow of the world. She smiled as she sang, her eyes looking from one to another of us, as though she were anxious above all else that we should miss nothing of what we

sang. We always sang just before the close a song
about a tree that stood in a wood. *Er steht ein
Baum im Odenwald,* it said. This tree had many
of the greenest of leaves upon it and a strange and
beautiful bird which sat quietly in its nest upon
the highest branch. There was more in the song
which I have now forgotten, but I remember a
lover and his sweetheart, snow *so kalt, so kalt,* and
a broken heart. I have never been able since to find
this song in any collection of German songs, although it is doubtless familiar enough to those
who know them well. But the concentrated misery
either within or placed within the simple words
and music and the deep pleasure therein will always remain with me. As a last selection we always sang, *Komm, Herr Jesus, sei unser Gast,*
walked in the garden for a few minutes, and went
to bed.

Everybody at *das Elsterhaus* had a birthday during his stay regardless of its actual date. This was
an innovation of Fräulein Trobitsius, who, like all
normal persons, loved to show off. These birthday
suppers were allotted in advance, and we all
dressed up for them. We sang birthday songs and
wished well in all manner of speaking to the recipient of the party, who sat at the head of the
table with a wreath of flowers around his head.
Fräulein Trobitsius brought in her cake at the
close of supper with a flourish. It was her high mo-

ment when life was most strong within her, and we all rejoiced in her triumph.

I have since searched in many corners of the earth for a cake like Fräulein Trobitsius' *Geburts-tagskuchen;* but I have not found it, not in London or New York, Paris or Brussels, not even in Vienna or Munich, at the most original of confectioners and caterers. Perhaps this is not odd since each cake was in a sense made to order. On the morning of the birthday feast Fräulein Trobitsius always asked the recipient of her art to name his favorite story from Andersen or Grimm. Then with a swift clatter in the kitchen she began her creation. Hansel and Gretel were done in pink and blue sugar, the witch in green; the little mermaid had her tail set in jewels; twelve white swans clustered about Elsa. The cake, three tiers high, came in with a lighted candle on its top, borne by Fräulein Trobitsius in an ample white apron, while we rose and shouted birthday songs and then crowned its maker with flowers.

All things good and wholesome were in *das El-sterhaus*. Merriment and sadness met there together as in all well-ordered homes. I shall never go back to Blankenburg; but I shall know it always as possessing a corner of this earth where people were born again in spirit.

When I came away, Fräulein Elster presented me with a picture of *das Elsterhaus* upon the back of which she had written:

"Nur freundliche Erinnerungen begleiten Dich und immerlastende Freundschaft von einem land zum andern."

("Only fond remembrances go with you and friendship forevermore from one land to another.")

Chapter VII

LIFE IN MONTANA

VII

WHEN I look back on my second and last year at Mrs. Moffat's, I am never able to divide its weeks and months into separate and vivid periods of time. I am sure that things went on in their same ordered, yet frenzied way. I know that we kept up our assiduous correspondence and that I listened to Mrs. Moffat's midnight thoughts and schemes. I know that I taught my German far better because of Fräulein Franke's Prussianism and the warm reality of Fräulein Elster's kindness. I gave up my graduate study at Chicago because of the lack both of time and of sufficient energy.

I was, in fact, ill most of the time during my second year at Mrs. Moffat's, although neither she nor I recognized this fact. Mrs. Moffat hated illness. She said that the sight of impaired physical or mental powers was not only painful to her but in an odd sense distasteful. She was visibly annoyed by the cough which I had in some unknown way contracted in Germany and which all her advice and concoctions could not cure. Neither she nor I could understand why I grew so thin with all the good food she so amply provided for us all.

My father died in February of 1914 after a long and terrible illness. I was in Maine for a fortnight before he died, a fortnight of almost constant northeast snowstorms, which banked our great old house and made sickness and death seem even more inexorable. When I returned to Chicago and waited for the long, slow spring, I realized that for the first time in my relatively short life I could be so completely exhausted that even my problematical future held no interest for me.

After two months at home in the summer, months spent chiefly in coughing, I was sent in August upon the insistence of certain good, if annoying, doctors to the Rocky Mountains. There had been hurried conferences as to just where I should go, and the decision had at last fallen to a town in Montana called Bozeman. This town meant little to me although a college friend of mine lived there, her husband being a member of the faculty of the Montana State College. Her presence there meant that I should not be entirely among strangers; the altitude of Bozeman possessed the seemingly requisite thousands of feet; and, above all else, the specialist who had sealed my fate knew an excellent doctor in that town who would look out for me.

I shall always remember my arrival in Bozeman. I reached there in the late afternoon of

August twenty-second and in a driving snowstorm.
I had been journeying for hours through brown,
sun-baked country with spurs of mountains lying
here and there, as though in some long-past up-
heaval of nature they had been hurled from the
higher ranges in the distance to fall upon the barren land. Now and then this barren land had given
place to acres upon acres of harvested ground,
some set about with shocks of grain, some bare,
and so wide in extent that the houses and barns
beyond them looked diminutive and insignificant
by very contrast. There were miles, too, of rolling, tumbling foot-hills, brown, and shaven close
by innumerable herds of cattle. The warm, summer sunlight lay over all, so that to come suddenly
into gray obscurity and driving snow held something of terror in its suddenness.

2

Bozeman in 1914 was a small city of some seven
thousand people, set in the fertile valley of the
Gallatin River with mountains towering on every
side. I had never before seen a mountain higher
than the Harz or the Mt. Desert hills, and for
some days I was at a loss to know whether I should
be awed or comforted by them. Long before I had
lived three years among them I discovered either
emotion, or even a combination of the two, quite
insufficient.

In 1914 the State of Montana still had its open ranges. Here it was easy to picture the scriptural cattle upon a thousand hills and quite as easy to assume their belonging to God since there was no other visible owner about. In 1914 there was also land still open for homesteading; and I have never quite recovered from the urge I had then to live in a shack at the corner of some great piece of land which would ultimately become my own. Automobiles were rare in Bozeman in those days. Ranchers drove in from their homes throughout the valley in cumbersome rigs and through clouds of summer dust to do their trading. Cowboys in chaps were a common sight as was their uproar on Saturday nights a common sound.

I never grew either accustomed to or tired of the weather in the Gallatin Valley. Hazlitt says somewhere that an interest in weather is the final resource of the end of a life spent in study. Life was still strong within me, ill as I was; far from its end, I hoped and believed; and yet Montana weather became a resource in itself and remained so during my three years there. Reared as I had been by the sea and weatherwise as all coast people are, I was constantly baffled by mountain weather. Fair days followed fair days, sometimes for a month at a time, motionless days of high, clear sunshine, nights of innumerable stars. It would never rain again, I thought. Then, with seemingly no warning, a warm wind blew from the Pacific over the

mountain ranges to the west, and long streamers
of rain came in its wake.

I never grew used to the winter cold. It held
a terror there as in no other place I have ever
known. Sometimes for days at a stretch we were
smitten by bitter cold, cold twenty degrees and
more below zero, wrapped and hooded in it, almost suffocated by it. There was something terrifying in the way this sharp, dry cold seemed to
descend from the mountains, fall in icy streams
from the winter sky, to lie upon the submissive
earth. When one went to bed at night, one saw the
cold from one's windows, ruthless, engulfing, cruel.
I have never forgotten the sense of helplessness
before it.

Then on a bitter, brilliant February day, when
we had been held for weeks in an icy vise, when
our nerves were taut with a strange fear, the temperature would suddenly start to rise. It leapt up
by quick degrees, fifty sometimes in a few hours,
and by nightfall the air would be soft with a false
promise of spring and a warm rain would begin
to fall. A "chinook" they called this wind. It was
a blessing to one's mind as well as to one's shiver-
ing, nervous body.

3

Before I had been a week in Bozeman, my doctor, whom I liked as I have liked few persons
and to whose care and common sense I owe bless-

ings incalculable, suggested that I go out into the country upon a cattle ranch which he knew for a stay of some weeks. This ranch, known as the Wilson ranch, was high in the foothills of the Rockies, some ten miles from town and three miles from any neighbors. The ranch house, which lay in a depression among the hills, was small and inconsiderable although comfortable enough. Numberless corrals for cattle shelters at branding-time or in bad weather stretched beyond it. A barn or tool-shed stood near at hand across the small dooryard.

I always had the odd and sometimes uneasy feeling on the Wilson ranch that others besides Mrs. Wilson, her daughter of my age, and some migratory cattle-hands were with us; in fact, I could have sworn to any number of invisible presences about the place. Perhaps this conviction of mine arose from the personality of Mrs. Wilson herself. She was a silent woman with large staring dark eyes which were always gazing into some unfamiliar distance. She literally never spoke unless occasion demanded it. She gave me numberless fresh eggs and gallons of milk while I sojourned with her; but those completed her offerings. Her daughter rode the range most of the day on some mysterious business with the cattle, and when she was within the house paid as little attention to me as did her mother.

I was rarely within the house myself. The September days succeeded one another, clear, flawless, with no hint of rain. I have never seen such steady, golden light over any land as over our wide sweep of hills and mountains. Beyond the corrals and through a narrow gulch I could easily reach the side of a hill on the open range where a small enclosure of iron fence-posts marked the grave of some "old-timer" buried there years before. This burial-place was seemingly made for my purposes. It held the sun from ten until four o'clock; it was securely fenced from roaming cattle; and its raised grave and slanting tomb-stone formed a comfortable couch and a rest at just the proper angle for my back.

I spent most of my days on the Wilson ranch on this grave. I read most of the morning, swallowed two eggs at noon, drank my milk from a small stone jar, and ate several chicken sandwiches provided by Mrs. Wilson. After my lunch I took a nap lying with my head in the short grass and with the sun warm upon my back. The coloring of the hills and mountains about and above enchanted me as the day wore on. It was impossible to discover the source of the shadows which stalked over them since there were almost never clouds in the sky. In the hollows and depressions among them yellow quaking-aspens and brilliant red service-berry bushes flamed by hidden streams. Sounds of distant cattle broke the still air now and then, and, if one listened carefully, the running of water in numerous mountain creeks.

I did not like the short evenings at the Wilson ranch, but I loved the nights. I slept out-of-doors on an army cot in the corral that surrounded the house. When I was once settled there, deep below my blankets, I wanted for nothing. The air was cold and clear; the stars were numberless. The silence did not so much lie over the earth or surround it as it enfolded and enveloped it. It seemed to come steadily down from the mountains above like an engulfing stream until it had covered everything and become one with sleep.

On these nights before I slept I thought of Gabriel Oak on Norcombe Hill. The sky, its September constellations, the Great Bear, Cassiopeia, and the Northern Cross, seemed timed by one common pulse, and, as I lay still, I could feel the roll of the world eastward and watch my steady progress through the stars.

4

Had I known when I went to the Rocky Mountains how long my stay would be among them, I should doubtless have felt vastly sorry for myself. But, as a matter of fact, even after I had begun to realize that it might be a long time before I could again turn my steps eastward, I was having a very good time of it. In the first place, I had never before been thrown upon my own mental resources with no pressure from without, never before, as Mrs. Abbie Moffat would have piously said, been "master of my own fate." Here in Montana for the first time in my life people began to assume positions of relatively little importance in my existence. By the very fact of being ill I was naturally set more or less apart from them and from their multifarious activities. This resulted, rather to my surprise, not in a sense of deprivation but rather in an exciting sense of freedom. My long days were mine as they had never been mine before, and I set about enjoying them to the full.

I could always read even in a cold room with open windows; and as the winter in town came on and I found myself with pleasant people who left me very much alone, I began to read for long, uninterrupted hours. I kept on with my German, renewed my Latin and Greek, read poetry, drama, philosophy, and fiction. In those long, quiet days and evenings I lived in a world far more real than I had ever known it to be, a vast, immeasurable world, whose height, breadth, and depth had been created by others greater than I for people like me. Before, I had read largely for incident, situation, and sentiment; now, hardly knowing it, I read for thought and meaning, vision and wisdom. I became in that winter literally intoxicated with books and with thoughts, half grasped, perhaps, but leading on and on into mazes of speculation. I divided my months into weeks, a week of Hardy, a week of Shakespeare, a week of Pater. I read *Marius the Epicurean* that winter, holding it in my mittened hands, reading it aloud in my still room, excited beyond all excitement by its music. I discovered Dante in Montana, the metaphysical poets, the dialogues of Plato. These books, many of which I had seemingly read before, now became mine forevermore by the very miracle of undistracted time.

Fiction took on new light in that long winter of reading. It ceased to be a chronicle of events and situations, of characters interesting or dull as the case might be. It came to be a many-faceted outlook on life, created and propelled by thoughts and ideas rather than by incidents and action. I read *The Brothers Karamazov* for the first time, *Anna Karenina,* and *The Way of all Flesh; Diana of the Crossways, The Mayor of Casterbridge,* and *Madame Bovary.* "We begin to live," says Yeats, "when we have conceived life as a tragedy." I do not know that I had ever heard it said at that time, or even if it had been said in those words; but I could then have understood its meaning as never before: not as a dark thought, but rather as a bright one, touched with humanity, filled with pity and understanding, embracing the world with wisdom.

I had other pastimes that winter besides my

reading. On a long square table in the corner of my room I had a large map of Europe tacked securely to its edges. I had colored pins for opposing forces, which I moved day by day or week by week as I consumed the latest despatches of the War. This exercise, rueful as it was, took on the excitement of a game. I was much distressed in late autumn by a letter from Fräulein Elster in which she begged me to understand her distress and to be as kind as I could toward accusations against her country. No letter ever came to me from Fräulein Franke.

I began to write that winter, sometimes imitating styles and diction which I liked, sometimes striking out for myself in simpler fields. I had dreams of writing a novel based on one of a dozen new ideas which I had gained from my reading; but the consciousness of my own immaturity held me back. In 1915 twenty-eight was a far younger age than it is today; and I at twenty-eight was far younger than most of that age. I began, therefore, to write a story for girls of fourteen or thereabouts and continued with it for two hours daily throughout the winter. When in April it was accepted for publication by a Boston firm and I received a check for one hundred and fifty dollars, I sincerely believed that the world of literary achievement and success lay at my feet!

I remember how, when I had found the letter with the check in my post-office box, I stood on the street longing for some acquaintance to pass by so that I might electrify him with my good tidings. The few persons whom I knew being else-where, I sent a telegram to my mother and then proceeded to consume great quantities of chocolate ice-cream all by myself in an ugly restaurant. This delicious fare has always been my indulgence, whenever procurable, in all hours of triumph!

5

I had not been a month in Montana before strength began to return to me. At first it came like the hardly perceptible motion of the tide creeping over brown flats. Then, as October gave place to November, it came hurrying on like the racing waters on a full spring moon. I could feel it flooding my body, driving away weakness and pain. I recognized it in the new ease with which I held my book, in the new spring in my legs upon my daily walk, in new comfort and security at night. Milk and eggs, beef and butter, fruit and cream began to cover up my bones. One hundred and eighty fresh eggs a month, I thought, even at a cost of four dollars and fifty cents, were prov-ing to be worth the ghastly swallowing of them. The vulgar, according to Pope, imitating Horace, boil eggs; the learned roast them; but I had the compensation of neither the vulgar nor the learned! By the time the slow spring had loosened the streams in the canyons, I felt strong and peculiarly new in body and in mind. I had discovered like Hazlitt and Mrs. Blodgett that I was never less alone than when alone. Like Hazlitt, too, in *On Going a Journey* I wanted to run, leap, and sing for joy. My doctor, although he did not encourage the running, said I might ride if I wished; and for ten dollars a month I procured the companionship and labor of an Indian "cayuse" called Siwash. Siwash, like Rozinante, was thin and angular in spite of good feeding. He was likewise of a contemplative nature, peaceable upon most occasions, and quite unremarkable for speed. He seemed framed for my purposes, and I rode him for miles over mountain trails and through canyons.

The mountain flowers proved a source of great delight to me: the forget-me-nots by the streams, the lupines covering sandy slopes, the white columbines, penstemon, and hare-bells, the Indian paint brush, half flame, half feather. I loved the hot June sun on miles of silver-gray sagebrush, the clear outlines of the mountains, thin and sharp in the bright distance, as though one could sit astride them and touch the sky.

I spent the summer months in a mountain camp called Cold Spring, on the West Gallatin, miles from anywhere at all. I made friends with prospectors and cattle men, their faces filled with weather, their hands marked by work, and with the few other sojourners at Cold Spring, who had come up to the West Gallatin to fish. The days were long and often pleasantly hot, clear with the transparency of still, sunshot water; the nights were clear and cold. Sudden snow flurries came over us more often than rain.

That summer in my screened cabin on the west fork of the Gallatin with the sound of swift water always in my ears I read certain of the English essayists. I thought I had read many of their essays before, but I now discovered that I had never really done so. A friend had sent them to me in small volumes which I could carry, one or two at a time, in my pocket. I read Lamb with new pleasure, Hazlitt with admiration and sympathy, De Quincey with a passion of excitement and wonder. Pater again delighted my ears and satisfied me with other good things. I memorized certain sentences, which I liked because of their rhythm and diction, and said them over to myself on my walks or after I had gone to bed at night.

She was tumbled early by accident or design into a spacious closet of good old English reading and browsed at will upon that fair and wholesome pasturage.

No dignity is perfect which does not at some point ally itself with the mysterious.

And those simple gifts, like other objects as trivial, bread, oil, wine, milk—had regained for him, by their use in such religious service, that poetic

and as it were moral significance, which surely
belongs to all the means of daily life, could we but
break through the veil of familiarity with things
by no means vulgar in themselves.

It was on the tenth of April, 1798, that I sat
down to a volume of the New Eloise at the inn at
Llangollen, over a bottle of sherry and a cold
chicken.

I knew by the time I had finished and re-read
many of them that prose was more to me than
poetry. One expected beauty in poetry; the very
name assured one of it; but when an equal beauty
was discovered in prose, the discovery was that
much more exciting and satisfying. I was intrigued
by the thought, doubtless old to many but new to
me, that ordinary words, carelessly used in everyday speech, could, with no help of meter or of
rhyme, with no form already set for them, be endowed with such distinction and meaning that they
became both music and poetry.

Words began to fascinate me, their choice and
combination, their sound and color, their height
and depth, the possibilities within them of rhythm
and movement. Like Stevenson I began to imitate:
to try to write in honest yet vivid monosyllables
like Hazlitt; to use participles like Pater's; to
frame my sentences so that they would make one
conscious of a great height like De Quincey's. My
attempts were poor enough in all truth; but they
served to prove to me that in the study and teach-

ing of English prose, rather than of philosophy or history, I wanted to spend my days.

Yet I knew the time for that was years away. A long apprenticeship was first in order. I was poorly trained in English literature at best, and my very desire to specialize in my new discovery meant graduate study before the least of colleges would see fit to take a chance on me. Moreover, I had no money. All the little I had earned on my book had been converted into eggs and milk and duly swallowed. Much more had been borrowed. I must teach again as soon as I was able and in any position I could secure.

I am sure that the English essayists had themselves added to my new health and strength both by their words and sentences and by the vision of my future which they had given me. Now I knew the truth of Socrates' advice to the young Charmides when he remarks that headaches are cured easily by the cure of the soul, and that the soul is cured by the charm of "fair words."

6

My doctor was insistent upon my not returning east for another year at least; pleading made not the slightest impression upon him; and in late August I returned to Bozeman to begin to seek another fortune. I found it in early September in the office of the superintendent of public schools.

Mr. Cunningham, the superintendent, was an angular, completely bald man, a Methodist, and a Christian. He was frankly sceptical of my fitness for public school teaching, and he said so in the kindest possible manner. Had my entrance into his office not coincided with the sudden and unexpected withdrawal of one of his teachers of English, had he not, as he told me, been a believer in Destiny, I am sure he would not have considered me for a moment. But since circumstances seemed to have placed me in his hands, he was disposed to take me for better or for worse. The position which he offered me was in the seventh and eighth grades of what was then known as departmental teaching; and, poor as I was, I accepted it as unwillingly as he offered it.

I fear that I did not enter upon my new position in September with any extra grace of spirit. I had never taught in a public school system and, with my new ambition warm and glowing within me, I did not wish to do so. But whatever grace I lacked on my first day in the Irving School was provided for me, pressed down and running over, by its principal.

Leora Hapner was a woman in her late thirties, perhaps, a Montana product and a native of Bozeman. She was not only one of the best teachers I have ever known, but she was also a genius at school management. She was, moreover, a woman of fine cultivation and finer spirit. She knew pre-

cisely of what stuff most of her three hundred children were made, and, accepting them for what
they were, she began to pull her school into order
and action after the inroads upon her charges of
a summer vacation. She was a fine-looking woman,
tall and thin, with an olive skin and arresting dark-
gray eyes. She looked, and was, honest and fair,
just and kind, energetic and resourceful. She was
a genius, too, at discipline. She knew how to speak
the language and get inside the minds of tall,
strapping youths from the ranges and ranches. She
could wield a wide leather strap across the knees
of unruly boys, who sat calmly in a chair without the least outcry and liked her while she was
doing it. Punishment of this sort, still not only
allowed but encouraged in Montana, at least,
seemed not to flurry her at all. She did not like it,
but she took it, as she took everything else, in her
stride.

There was every reason why she might not have
relished my entrance into her well-run school. I
had had neither training nor experience in public school teaching. I knew neither western children nor the social environment from which they
came. I was obviously using the school as a stop-
gap and interim before I should go into other
fields. I had been ill and conceivably might be ill
again. I was completely unknown to her and, for
all she knew, might have none of those qualities
which she required in her teachers.

If any of these deficiencies rendered my presence in the Irving School problematical to her, I was never for a moment conscious of the fact. From the day I walked into her office and was introduced by her to the other teachers, I had the odd, yet comfortable, feeling that I was exactly where I belonged. All the nonsense which had been in my mind, that to teach perhaps inferior youngsters of twelve and thirteen was a definite stepdown from what I had been doing and from what I wanted to do, vanished in her presence as the most unworthy of notions. I began at once to love my teaching, and I continued to do so as long as I remained in the Irving School.

I liked my associates also. They were mostly from the west; no one but me was from New England; but whatever suspicion they may have had of me was lost in the common friendliness engendered in the principal's office and disseminated throughout the school. Most of them were better teachers than I, for they were on their home ground, had had generous experience in public school teaching, and knew what was expected of them as I did not.

I afforded them amusement both by my ignorance and by my hand-writing, which could never fulfill Montana standards. We were all required to write according to the Palmer Method of Penmanship; in fact, until we had satisfied the chirographic ideas and ideals of Messrs. Palmer and

Company of Chicago, we each sacrificed every month five dollars of our salaries. Since my monthly pay check was only eighty dollars, I felt a righteous resentment at the five dollars docked each pay day because I could not write in a manner which I secretly despised; yet try as I would, I could never master the inditing of a certain sentence which proved conclusively to the Palmers whether or not we were possessors of their art. This sentence, which I practised daily under the tutelage of some good-natured teacher, already arrived at excellence, read

I am pining for a pin to use in pinning.

Since in the course of a year and a half I never learned to write it to the satisfaction of the Palmers, to whom I hopefully sent my efforts weekly, my salary remained at seventy-five dollars during my stay in the Irving School.

7

The work at the Irving was hard and from Monday to Friday never-ending. The school was organized to the last degree. From eight-thirty until four, we marched on, in time with bells and schedules. I taught six periods a day to classes of forty or fifty, English grammar in three periods, reading in three. When I was not teaching, I was in charge of a room of sixty boys and girls from thirteen to sixteen years of age, to most of whom school was merely to be tolerated and none too graciously tolerated at best.

I learned at once that the children of a mountain state were different in most respects from those of New England. Surely they resembled in nothing the boys and girls of Hillside and my affable, well-to-do little girls in Chicago. Montana in 1915 was still young. Its first settlers had come only fifty years before in the wake of gold suddenly discovered at Alder Gulch. There are few more potent magnets than gold to draw undesirables from one place to another; and in her early days Montana had her soldiers of fortune, adventurers, and ne'er-do-wells. The permanent settlers who followed the miners were of far better stock; they came for the most part from middle and southwestern states in search of farms and ranches and of whatever else a new land might offer; and yet the very fact that the new territory was in a state of actual blockade for several months under the control of its lawless elements proves something of the rigor of an existence which still boiled and bubbled in the active memory of hundreds of families.

The children, many of whom were of the first generation and none beyond the second, partook of the enterprise of their parents. They partook also of their energy and restlessness. Except for the few children of professional families, most of those whom I taught or strove to discipline in my crowded room cared little for books and nothing for study. Both seemed unrelated to cattle ranges and wheat ranches or even to many of their homes in town. They were lazy in certain ways, and yet resourceful, crude in certain ways, and yet instinctively decent. Some of them were lawless in the extreme. They loved courage and scorned weakness; they knew horses, cattle, and wheat, rattlesnakes, rifles, and round-ups. They were, like their parents, new people in a new state; and they had about them all the fearlessness and activity, all the strength and elasticity of a new and lively portion of the earth six thousand feet in the air. They were, in short, the most intensely physical, the most vitally alive, of any youngsters I had ever known; and high-pressure methods of dealing with them were the order of the day.

Needless to say, they thought English grammar the most senseless of subjects; and few of them saw any relation between it and their speech. Reading was acceptable if it had sufficient punch in it, but poems like "The Chambered Nautilus" were so much bunk that had to be learned and then were forgotten as quickly as possible. The rude bridge that arched the flood meant nothing to them; and the Pilgrim fathers on their stern and rockbound coast were pale and paltry enough when compared with Lewis and Clark and with Custer's Last Stand. My chief resource in their minds, my one

possession which they envied, was my knowledge
of the sea which few of them had ever seen. My
tales of shipwreck and pirates, which I told them
as a reward for decent behavior, lent to me my
chief value as their teacher.

There were, of course, notable exceptions among
them. Not all the sixty in my room were ignorant
of the so-called amenities of life. Wealth and substance had brought to several families advantages
which they were quick to seize upon for their
children. Among the hundred or so from other
rooms were boys and girls of college professors,
of doctors, lawyers, and ministers. One of my girls
now writes detective stories in New York. Several
of my boys are intelligent and well-educated
ranchers with books in their homes. Only last winter in San Francisco I met a young woman, once
in my room in the Irving School, now in an educational position of trust and responsibility.

But in my presentation of young Montana in
1915 I speak of the rank and file, for it was they
who made my teaching there distinctive and ad-
venturous. They somehow gave me an abiding respect for life quite outside of books, for physical
resourcefulness and vitality, for courage and rough
humor, and raucous abounding health. Some of
them rode into school from farms and ranches on
bitter mornings, stamping into my room with such
animation and spirit that I felt strong on the instant. What they lacked in tradition and back-

ground they made up for in a quite unconscious love of life and a basic kindliness characteristic of people in a wide, new land.

They little understood what they gave to me. The world in a curious way seemed new while I was among them. And although I could never have been satisfied to stay with them or with others like them, I carried away with me to the graduate school because of them, quite as much as the memory of illimitable country, the sense of basic, untutored natural excellence—in other words, a sense of those virtues and values which in the early ages of the world, when other lands were new, marked out gods and heroes and made them immortal in art and song.

8

I taught a year and a term in the Irving School without a dull moment. I grew strong like my youngsters and even physically resourceful to a certain degree. I rode hundreds of miles through Montana and Wyoming; I learned the ways of mountain camping; I became a fairly good shot with a rifle. Saturday and Sunday in fall and spring and all vacations found me in the canyons with or without others like-minded. I learned a great deal about birds and flowers, a little about geology, much about weather.

I had, or at least took, little time to read during

my last two years in Bozeman. The memory of
my long year spent with books was still warm
within me, ready to be built upon again when the
time should come. But my days were too filled
with a life outside individual study for me to accomplish much therein. In odd hours during the
two years I wrote another book, as lacking in distinction as the first.

In December of my last year I moved from
the Irving School to the Gallatin County High
School where a teacher of history and English
was suddenly needed. The work was more advanced; the problem of discipline less vigorous;
and the experience all to the good. My students
there were of basically the same type as in the
Irving School although the forcibly fed had
largely eliminated themselves. I grew to know well
certain of my boys and girls, visited several of
them on their ranches, and enjoyed them to the
full.

I left Bozeman in the spring of 1917 to enter
the University of Minnesota in the autumn as a
graduate student. I have never been back, but I
shall go some day to render tribute where tribute
is due. From time to time I see certain of my
friends who taught there with me and laugh with
them about pining for pins. Occasionally one of
my former students appears in one or another corner of the country. The principal of the Irving
School, to whom I owe more than I can ever re-

pay, is now on the faculty of Montana State College as a teacher of economics. I feel sure she understands with me that in the liveliness, rigor, and fun of the Irving School we gained resources incalculable for graduate study and for college teaching.

THE UNIVERSITY OF MINNESOTA

VIII

MY CHOICE of a graduate school had been in a large measure forced upon me by my doctor. He refused to consider Chicago with its dirt and smoke; he advised strongly against the fogs and sea-level of New England. If a suitable graduate school in a mountain climate did not exist, he said, then he was willing to compromise on one in a northern, inland location. Since I was completely cured, strong and well, his restrictions were irritating; and yet I was forced to agree with him that discretion in this case was the better part of valor.

The state of Minnesota was in high favor with him, and fortunately for me its university was second to none. I accordingly decided on Minneapolis as my next place of residence, and in the spring of 1917 put in my application for a graduate fellowship. I felt pleasantly reckless as I did so. I had very little money and was still in debt, but ambition set at naught all practical considerations. I have always been given throughout my life to odd so-called "hunches", and the "hunch" that I should go to Minnesota and that all would be well led me to put out of my mind purely empirical anxieties and necessities. This tide in my affairs, I thought, must be taken at its flood and would inevitably lead on to fortune.

If the Committee on Graduate Study at the University of Minnesota could have known me and my inadequate assets for a graduate school, I should never have met favor with them even to the extent of free tuition and a scholarship grant of two hundred and fifty dollars a year. I had been poorly trained in English at a small and, then, quite undistinguished college. I had been eight years away from concentrated study, and what teaching I had done, most of it not in English, had been too elementary to further my stock in trade. I had read fairly widely and at least during my first year in Montana with a passion of excitement and wonder; yet those who know graduate schools realize all too well that excitement and wonder are not rated so highly by them as sound knowledge and basic information.

I am sure I never sat down with paper and pencil to discover if any miraculous computation of twenty-five dollars a month plus two hundred dollars which I had saved (and owed) could feed, clothe, and sleep a graduate student for one year. I have never, in fact, been drawn toward financial computations of any sort. I had the vaulting notion that what I lacked in money I would earn by writing, and, as it happened, that is precisely what I did do.

Since the better monthly magazines of the country had one and all failed to appreciate my wares, I turned to humbler fields. In the spring and summer of 1917 I began avid composition for all manner of Sunday-school papers upon all manner of uplifting subjects. Lutheran, Baptist, Methodist, Presbyterian, Congregational, Unitarian publications for the young became grist to my mill; and by September I had induced a syndicate of certain of these to purchase an inspiring weekly article on some book, old or new, for their young readers at ten dollars an article. I should, in fact, never have subsisted my first year in the graduate school without the American Sunday-school, and I here and now accord it my grateful thanks.

2

In St. Paul's epistle to the Romans there is an acknowledgment which, I have lately thought, might well be placed above the entrance to all American graduate schools, even alas! to the most honorable among them:

I am debtor both to the wise, and to the unwise.

Graduate students might then apprehend at once what the best among them all too soon discover to be their fate.

For I have become persuaded both by direct and by indirect evidence that the worst teaching known to all ages and states of learning is at present perpetrated in certain of our graduate schools and that the nadir of this teaching is found in the fair fields of English literature. Just why these things should be true I have not been able to discover. That they are true I am convinced beyond the shadow of a doubt.

Too many scholars in the realms of English literature seem to their students strangely damaged by their subject. Their really wide and profound erudition has, paradoxically enough, one would think, rendered them oddly ill-nourished. Like Keats' knight-at-arms they are too often "alone and palely loitering". If they were ever enthralled by fancy, the spell is still their own and quite incommunicable. In their teaching they lack what Hazlitt terms *gusto* in any form. Surely they seemingly have no "power or passion" in presenting to their students those things which they have discovered and presumably loved through years of study. Consumed with interest though they may be, that interest is too seldom allowed to escape in their seminars and class-rooms. Their knowledge is always apparent; their excitement effectually concealed. Indeed, I have more than once thought that the fine words from *Samson Agonistes,* if one longed to be ironic, might well characterize too many lecturers in our graduate schools: *Calm of mind, all passion spent.* John Milton further and aptly describes their teaching: *No light but darkness visible.*

I have come, in fact, to the sad conclusion that great erudition is too often clothed in dullness, that the most learned teachers are too often the most benumbing. Vividness and vitality in the presentation of one's subject seem somehow in the minds of scholars to be out of place in a graduate school, qualities too closely associated with life outside of books to be allowed entrance therein. The rare teacher, who manages to infuse personality into his lectures, who in the minds of his students will be remembered for what he was rather than for what he taught, is too often looked upon with suspicion by his colleagues in the graduate school. Popularity with one's students, it would seem, has no place there. There enthusiasm and interest are synonymous with superficiality and playing to the gallery. Vision, that power of awakening the imagination, of exciting one's students to know more and more, of communicating the spell under which one has lived and studied—this it is that makes great teaching. And this it is which is too often sadly lacking in those whose work it is to train graduate students for college teaching.

Pater in *Marius the Epicurean* has a definition

of higher education which, although it would scandalize many professors in graduate schools, still seems sound to me. He says that the chief function of all higher education is "to impart the art of so relieving the ideal or poetic traits, the elements of distinction, in our everyday life—of so exclusively living in them—that the unadorned remainder of it, the mere drift and debris of our days, comes to be as though it were not." Surely no subject of study is more rich in elements of distinction than is English literature; and yet often the unadorned remainder seems to weigh more heavily in the minds of scholars. It is surely true that vision without knowledge is unstable and unwise; but it is just as surely true that knowledge without vision is barren and useless. Unless a scholar has both in his study and in his teaching some sense of adventure, some gleam to cast upon untravelled worlds of the mind and the spirit, his study and his teaching are alike dead forevermore.

Graduate students then are debtors both to the wise and to the unwise, and too often to the latter. It is small wonder that splendid college teachers, even today when our graduate schools are swarming, are hard to find. Too many of them become so mad after mere knowledge and after emulating the dispensers of it that they are unable through the rest of their days to free themselves from its incubus. "He who is still under the spell, and he who has never felt the spell", writes Amiel, "are equally incompetent." Although Amiel was not writing of American graduate schools, their professors and their products, no better comment could be made upon them.

3

I hasten now to absolve the Graduate School of the University of Minnesota from any such imputations on graduate schools in general. At Minnesota I was debtor only to the wise. During the five years I studied there I had no unwise, incomplete teachers, none damaged by their subject, none ill-nourished and "palely loitering". In fact, I know now as I knew then, that no graduate school in the country has ever gathered together, at least in the field of English, a more splendid staff of scholars and teachers. I was a miserable flint-head enough for their bright steels; but, immature and untrained as I was, I never knew a dull moment under their teaching and direction.

A number of circumstances made me decide, after I had taken my master's degree in English in 1918, to take four years instead of two to complete my doctorate. Our entrance into the World War was one of these, this colossal, fateful event changing the trend even of my little life. Before 1917 was far on its course many young men on the instructorial staff were entering the service. This left classes in Freshman English without teachers;

and early in 1918 I was offered a part-time instructorship in that subject to take the place of a man who had enlisted. In the autumn of 1918 I began full-time teaching as an instructor and carried half the normal program of a graduate student at the same time.

I have always felt that full-time graduate study unrelieved by any other sort of work is likely to be cumbersome and unwholesome in its effects. I have always been glad that my financial situation made the acceptance of an instructorship imperative. To teach twelve hours a week, to read ninety freshman themes, hard as it was, made my graduate study all the more exciting. To have to make time for any valuable pursuit in life only makes the pursuit more valuable. Moreover, my association with students in the class-room gave a wholesome balance to my study which in turn enriched my teaching. I was, in other words, learning as I taught, both learning and teaching contributing one to the other.

No college graduate today who unwisely enters any graduate school immediately after the bachelor's degree can possibly enjoy and profit by advanced study as I did in my five years at the University of Minnesota. My study was the fulfillment of years of desire. I had a perspective upon it gained alike from seven years of teaching and from one of illness. Even my very academic unfitness for it made it all the more entrancing when it came at last. My teachers seemed to me, and, indeed were, the best that I could have found, and I studied under their direction in a glow of excitement.

I worked in Shakespeare and Elizabethan Drama under Elmer Edgar Stoll, known throughout this country and elsewhere as one of the most original and basic of Shakespearean scholars. Mr. Stoll was (and still *is*) a charming man as well. As his assistant, I read papers for him my first year and because of that came into pleasant association with him. His teaching was sound and thorough; none could have been more so; but it was also shot through and through with personal excitement and fervor. Surely he came to his task "as to a sport". He could make the question of delay in *Hamlet* far more fascinating than a detective story, the women in the comedies far more charming than women elsewhere. Mr. Stoll, in fact, had sound and zealous notions on the attractiveness of women in general, in or out of Shakespeare. His favorite lines descriptive of feminine beauty were those of Spenser which picture Belphoebe in *The Faerie Queene:*

Upon her eyelids many Graces sate
Under the shadow of her even browes.

He had proved the soundness of his judgment in his wise selection of a wife; and he held, sanely enough, that certain perils lay for young women in too much learning. I always felt that by looking my best in his presence I was doing a service to all of our sex engaged in the costly pursuit of a doctor's degree.

I studied the history of the drama with Oscar Firkins, whose death a few years ago took from us one of the most brilliant of American critics. I was terrified of Mr. Firkins from my first embarrassed entrance into his office, when I discovered him curled into a ball with Euripides behind a huge arm-chair in a corner, until I retired with no flying colors from his instruction. He was a tiny, near-sighted man in thick spectacles; and he never recognized anyone in his immediate neighborhood if he could possibly avoid doing so. He lived with his three sisters, who, rumor had it, went about the house in bedroom slippers to avoid disturbing him while he was at work. If this was true, I wonder that they were ever properly shod except when he was out of the house, for he was always at work. He seemingly had no friends and loved the pleasant lack of them. His English was at once meticulous and elegant in his writing as well as in his speech, as his fine book on Jane Austen bears witness. He was the most brilliant of lecturers, and his finished sentences contained such niceties of expression that one never dared miss a word or phrase. He was at his best, I thought, on Greek tragedy. While he lectured, he paced the small platform of his class-room in a fine frenzy, weaving back and forth in a sidling motion like Coleridge. I always, indeed, thought of Lamb's apostrophe to Coleridge in *Christ's Hospital Five and Thirty Years Ago* when he recited Greek verse; for his accents from his platform were, I felt sure, as inspired as those of the charity boy reciting Pindar and Homer in the cloisters of the old Gray Friars. He had an odd and painful way as he lectured of bending far back the third finger of his left hand with the third finger of his right. I have always been physically sensitive to gestures of this sort, and my own left hand was in actual torment during most of the two hours.

My professor of Anglo-Saxon was Frederick Klaeber, well-known to most graduate students in English everywhere by his edition of the *Beowulf*. He was a marvellous teacher, making a subject that might have been dull enough full of color and light. He saw no reason in the world why everyone should not be madly in love with linguistics, which were seemingly his one and only passion. He, too, was a small man, and he wore a tailed coat which reached below his knees and was always getting in his way. He had no sense of grades, which was not strange since he lived with Aelfric, King Alfred and the Venerable Bede; and once when he had accorded my one perfect paper a C and I remonstrated with him, he looked at me vaguely with his small blue eyes and said,

"Why do you mind? Those letters, they are nothing."

I studied linguistics further under Kemp Malone, now at Johns Hopkins; at least, I *think* his subject was linguistics, although, as a matter of delightful fact, I never really knew. He was a young man of my own age, and like Mr. Klaeber so completely sold on his own subject that while one was with him, one really did not need to know what he was talking about. He exemplified what Goethe says of Winckelmann: "One learns nothing when one reads him, but one becomes something." The *vivida vis animi* which we caught in Kemp Malone's seminar was far better than anything we learned, or did not learn. He saw no reason why anyone of us should not master enough Danish in a day or two to read a learned article in that language; and he was always making assignments for reading in quite unknown tongues. We were friends outside the seminar since we ate in the same house, and he was the best of companions since the love of life and the love of linguistics were to him one and the same thing. He had the kind of humor which I particularly liked. Once when we had gone to church together on Easter Sunday to listen to the worst of sermons, he pointed to a deaf old lady in the seat ahead of ours who had an ear-trumpet held tightly to her head.

"Incredible!" he whispered to me. "Can you

imagine why anybody should listen to this stuff
who doesn't have to?"

I studied the eighteenth century novel with
Cecil Moore, one of the best of scholars in that
field. He was a Southerner who had come from
Harvard to Minnesota, and he was far more a man
of the world than the hero of Mackenzie's novel
by that name which we read with him. He was by
all odds the worst driver of any of my teachers.
We rose at dawn to read novels and went to bed
with them at night. His lectures were so packed
with facts that we were exhausted after two hours
of writing them down; but since, like my father,
a fact to him glowed with life everlasting, the exercise was worth the exhaustion. He held us in our
reading for the most trivial of incidents, seemingly
the most unimportant of conversations; and he
had that genius characteristic of the best teachers
of making us slave for him and like it. He wore
brown suits and always smelled pleasantly of tobacco to which he was monstrously addicted. He
laughed uproariously upon all meet occasions;
and his laughter had a way of staying in the air
long after he had finished with it. I owe to him
my own pleasure in teaching the history of the
novel at Smith College; and whatever my own students have learned from me, they really owe to
him. Whenever we begin *Tom Jones* at Smith, I
pour out a libation in spirit before him. For he

never tired of Squire Western and the Seagrims whom he made immortal by great gusts of laughter.

Joseph Warren Beach was my teacher both in the essay and in the nineteenth century novel. He is known, or should be, to many of my readers for his book on Thomas Hardy, the best yet written, for his study of Henry James, and for his more recent books, *The Twentieth Century Novel* and *The Concept of Nature in Nineteenth Century Poetry*. Mr. Beach was (and fortunately *is*) a tall, thin man who always seemed to be in a terrific hurry. When he and his wife went walking, as they often did, he with his stick was always several paces ahead of her. He was always running in the university halls as though he had just lost sight of something and must regain it at all costs. Even in his class-room and seminar he was never really still. If he was not tearing up pieces of paper or breaking chalk into bits, he was running his fingers madly through his curly yellow hair. His mental activity was of a piece with his physical; indeed, I always thought he exemplified Pliny's contention that the agitation of the body excites the mind. He was forever being seized with a new idea in his class-room which made him jump suddenly in his chair or wave his hands in the air before he communicated it to us. Sometimes before he was really through with the first idea, another would attack him. But he always managed to sort them out at last. He had an intriguing way of announcing that there was probably nothing in these ideas at all. Take them or leave them, he said. But the very suddenness with which he made this announcement, together with the ideas themselves, gave his courses an atmosphere of "wild surmise" which entranced us all. Since new planets were always swimming into our ken in his lectures, this atmosphere of "wild surmise" seems the best way to characterize them.

I wrote my doctoral thesis on Thomas Hardy under Mr. Beach's direction. Since he taught me most of what I know of this greatest of novelists, my own graduate students at Smith are indebted to him rather than to me.

I worked in medieval allegory and metrical romances with Carleton Brown, who had come from Bryn Mawr to Minnesota. He had large round blue eyes the exact color of chicory blossoms, and they glowed with an odd excitement over Chrétien de Troyes and the *Roman de la Rose*. Giles and Phineas Fletcher were to him far more alive than Sinclair Lewis and infinitely more valuable to the human mind and soul. The idea of writing a thesis on Thomas Hardy rather than on the influence of the miracles of the Virgin on certain forms of other medieval literature was both anathema and pain to him. I feel sure I sacrificed whatever respect he had for me by deciding to specialize in the prose of the eighteenth and nineteenth centuries. Carleton Brown's chief contribution to his graduate students was in his eyes, where the Middle Ages glowed. He was, in fact, so much in love with the Middle Ages that we willingly lived in them for three hours a week. His wife had a daughter while we were roaming about in the romances; and when the child was named Emily instead of Guinevere or Cressida, Thisbe or Iseult, we were troubled by his sudden inconsistency. Life had after all made inroads upon him, we felt. His contributions to scholarship are many and varied as all scholars and many students know; yet we who now never read his articles because of our own ignorance remember the glow in his eyes over Righteousness and Peace kissing each other, although the occasion for this pious salutation is long since extinct in our minds. Sir Gawain, he reminded us, was, like Antaeus, said to gain strength and power from the earth whenever he touched it. Carleton Brown did not need to touch the earth for strength and power so long as he had secure hold upon Sir Gawain.

I was enrolled for two pleasant years at Minnesota in a seminar in Writing taught, or perhaps better, directed, by Joseph Thomas, then chairman of the department of English. We met on Mondays from two to four, reading in turn whatever we had written. Mr. Thomas was at once the best and the most merciless of critics. He had sharp hazel eyes and a sharp wit as well. He had a passion for Swift which was understandable since they were cut from much the same sturdy cloth. I rewrote my short stories after he had torn them in pieces, and when I sold them, I always had the uneasy consciousness that he should have the money. He was as miserly in praise as he was prodigal in censure, and a glance of approbation from him was worth many a sleepless night. He held with the ancients that art is imitation and that the life in art is quite as valuable to the would-be writer as life outside it. This I have found since to be the chief of literary truths. In common with others in his seminar who are now known for their stories and poems, essays and novels, I owe to his criticism and encouragement most of what I have accomplished in my writing since then; and I shall send him a copy of this book so that he may be apprised both of this fact and of my gratitude.

Since Mr. Stoll directed my destinies in graduate study and since he possessed the invincible conviction that some knowledge of French literature was advisable in the study of English, I took a course in classical tragedy under Professor Colbert Searles of the department of Romance Languages. Mr. Searles was very patient with me, I think because we both came from Maine. Surely there could have been no other reason. There may be others from Maine with a command of the French language like his; but I have never met them, nor have I ever believed a flair for modern languages among natural New England endowments. Perhaps Mr. Searles felt impelled to disprove the lack of linguistic ability among Maine people because of his Christian name! Surely his Maine accent, unlike mine, was never apparent in his French. I have often since thought how my reading of French must have pained him. His course was excellent, but very costly to me since, when I had to read papers in the seminar, I felt it necessary to engage a tutor some days beforehand to coach me in pronouncing Racine and Voltaire. Even with the coaching I must have been a monstrous cross to the ears of the modern language majors; and I can only hope that legitimate amusement somewhat lightened the burden of the cross.

All of these men with the exception of Oscar Firkins, who perhaps is reciting Euripides elsewhere, of Frederick Klaeber, Kemp Malone, and Carleton Brown, are still making the destinies of graduate students in Minneapolis pleasant. When I hear graduate students today, even in better known graduate schools, denounce and deplore the teaching meted out to them, I still think how fortunate I was. For at Minnesota the value of the subject never exonerated the teacher from boredom. And I know of no graduate school in the country superior to that above the swift Mississippi where scholarship came from darkness into light and where students learned unconsciously how to teach.

The graduate students at Minnesota in my days

there represented all sorts and conditions of men and women. Yet then graduate study was not as it is today the star to every wandering bark of unproved worth. We had among us certain "odd fishes", to use Lamb's term, it is true, but not so many as in these times clutter up graduate seminars to drive other students crazy and to force teachers to awake occasionally to human tragedies before their eyes as well as in their books. Perhaps, indeed, the impotence of many graduate schools today lies as much in the calibre of graduate students as in the teaching of them. For seemingly anyone possessing a bachelor's degree from any miserable institution in the country can storm the walls of most graduate schools if he have but the desire and sufficient money.

Our few "odd fishes" only made graduate study more exciting since they lent humor to our days. I remember one bald man in particular who longed to make the subject of his doctoral dissertation the influence of women's tresses upon literature in general. He came to his research from one of the Dakotas, slightly encumbered with a wife and twin sons. They formed the most devoted of families, seemingly seldom apart, for when the father came to the seminar his wife and sons accompanied him as far as the entrance. I shall never forget the twins. They were bald, too, and at nine months had identical expressionless blue eyes and loose mouths. They always gazed at each other stolidly from opposite ends of their perambulator across a huge pile of their father's books. They were thus initiated early into the wide fields of research; and I have often wondered how they have developed and what influence this close proximity to learning has had upon them.

I took my orals on the fourteenth day of May in 1922. The day held for me in prospect "the dreaded name of Demogorgon" in Hazlitt's words; for my oral examination for the master's degree had been the most disgraceful of performances. In fact, I had been succinctly and quite justly informed by Mr. Beach that it bore the distinction of the worst examination ever passed within his memory. I cannot say that my doctor's oral left my ten kind examiners with any glow of pride or wonder; yet I hope I retrieved myself somewhat.

I remember it mostly because it was an expensive occasion for me. I completely demolished a new pair of silk stockings through rubbing one ankle against the other in my extreme nervousness; I tore a new handkerchief into bits; and I summarily ruined a new suit by working at a button until I had torn a jagged hole in its jacket. But when I left my generous persecutors and walked homeward, I realized suddenly that I had at last fulfilled an ambition of many years, and, what is more, that I had for five of those years lived in the most substantial and beautiful of worlds.

4

After the securing of my doctor's degree I was promoted to an assistant professorship and remained four more years at Minnesota. I have always been glad that, unlike many of my colleagues at a women's college, I have had the experience of university teaching. We had, of course, among our ten thousand students then at Minnesota all types of young men and women, representative of all types of background and environment. Some came from well-to-do, cultured families of native American stock in Minneapolis and St. Paul and in other centers throughout the Middle West. These represented much the sort of background represented in our eastern colleges. Many more from these towns and cities were of Scandinavian stock, the first generation in their families to seek a college education. Others of diverse ancestry came from small towns and from the country, Finnish students from the Iron Range, Swedes, Danes, Norwegians, and Icelanders from the farms. From the names in my class-books I should have said that at least fifty percent were of some Northern European blood, descendants of the immigrant peoples of fifty years ago.

A class in Freshman English at Minnesota contained students of varying backgrounds and varying abilities. Practically all were from Minnesota high schools, some well trained, more with but a mediocre preparation. Today a so-called General College takes care of those not distinctly fitted for college work; but in my day there was no such separation.

Reading themes at Minnesota meant more than a little correction of grammatical errors, not to say of rhetorical. Freshmen there, with some outstanding exceptions, of course, were far less well read than are my students at Smith. But there was a spur to teaching there that I have found nowhere else. Many boys and girls were working their way through college, and study to them was a matter of prime importance since they were paying for it themselves. They were waiters in restaurants and hotels, bell-boys, elevator operators, nurses to children, house-maids, furnace men, porters, janitors. One of my boys was even an undertaker's assistant! In the summer they worked at everything under the sun.

Teaching such students was a thrilling experience. One felt that one was building background as well as ministering to present intellectual needs. Uncouth boys from farms and small towns changed in speech, manners, and dress even in one short year. I remember one boy from the country who came to my freshman class with his coat lapels decorated with lodge emblems, Red Cross badges, and Sunday-school pins. He had the worst of hair-cuts and the most ill-fitting of ugly suits. He looked, and in a burst of confidence con-

fessed to me that he *felt,* awkward and out-of-
place even in a class that contained several others
not much more advantaged than he. Before he had
been a fortnight with us, he had proved that he
was made of good intellectual stuff. He wrote
English well, and he had a genius for mathematics.
His mathematics teacher, himself once a country
boy, took an interest in him which extended even
to clothes and a hair-cut. The pins began to dis-
appear one by one from his new coat. I asked him
to supper, and at his request a lesson in table manners followed. By his sophomore year he had become in manners, appearance, and bearing the
gentleman that he had before been in mind. He
began to take a leading part in college activities
and became one of the best liked and respected of
students. He graduated with honors, later took a
doctorate in mathematics, and is now professor
of that subject in one of our best colleges.

This objective manner of sizing oneself up, this
recognition of social deficiencies, this knowledge
of what one lacked yet could nevertheless acquire,
were characteristic of most students of sturdy yet
limited backgrounds and environments. One was
constantly seeing seniors who bore no resemblance
to themselves as freshmen. The great state universities, with all their academic problems arising
from ill-prepared students who can enter from
high schools without examination, specialize in
just such swift metamorphoses; and a teacher in

one of them has a social responsibility which allies teaching with life in an exciting and remunerative way.

The Scandinavian stock with which Minnesota is well populated has always afforded splendid university material. Students from Swedish, Danish, and Norwegian families had a tenacity which I have never found in others. They knew what they wanted and were out to get it. They were, moreover, fine physical specimens. I have always thought one of the major rewards and compensations of teaching to be the physical beauty that sometimes eases one's disposition and gives pleasure to one's hours in the class-room. There were young Norse gods and goddesses about the Minnesota halls; and not infrequently their very appearance spurred one on to make their minds worthy of their bodies.

5

As soon as my doctor's degree was out of the way and I had more time, I began to teach a night class in University Extension Work. I did this partly for extra money, mostly because it amused and interested me. In 1923 and the years immediately following, a mania for writing short stories was sweeping the country; and there was a demand in the University Extension Division for classes in that exercise and art.

I may say at once that my courses in the technique of the short story (if there is such a thing) dealt almost exclusively with the exercise rather than with the art. I had classes at night once a week, two years in Minneapolis, two years in St. Paul. Each class was two hours in extent, from eight until ten. Each came at the close of a busy day, and yet I was too much entertained by the avidness of my students to feel tired when I once faced my multifarious audience at eight o'clock.

To write of night-class teaching is an act of supererogation since the publication of *The Education of HYMAN KAPLAN*. Every teacher of University Extension work will bless forevermore the author of that inimitable book. Yet there were compensations in the midst of the amusement, itself a compensation. My students, who dreamed of seeing their stories in print and who looked upon me as the holder of the magic key to success, came from literally every walk in life. They were hairdressers, street-car conductors, society women, plumbers, book-keepers, stenographers, clergymen, mothers, public-school teachers, taxi-drivers, lawyers, tailors, nurses, shop-keepers, and the manager of a hotel, who had more material seething in his mind than he had either time or ability to put on paper.

Every member of my class wrote a short story a fortnight. Some were so fired by zeal that they wrote one weekly. I read short stories on street-cars and buses, at my meals, and in bed at night.

I have never read worse stories, published or un-published, than many of those written presumably under my direction. There were exceptions, of course, but an exception never more clearly proved a rule than it did in University Extension courses, especially in those dedicated to literary expression.

Fragments or parts of short stories which I often assigned as exercises in my class interested very few of my students. They wanted to write the whole matter at white heat. They resented writing only the opening sentences of a story, a conclusion, or a dramatic incident. Sometimes when things seemed going badly and the author of some story clearly resented my criticism or that of his classmates, I tried to lighten the atmosphere by such an assignment. I allotted fifteen minutes of time during which each was to write the opening sentences of one of the stories seething in his mind. Some of these beginnings were memorable. I remember one which said:

When Mrs. Thompson, an excitable woman, knew beyond the shadow of a doubt that her four-year-old daughter Maisie was down the well, she summoned Mr. Thompson, an elderly man, who was ploughing his back field, to render her assistance.

Most of my would-be writers cared nothing for writing as its own end. They longed to sell their stories, and many of them, I fear, were grievously disappointed in me as a teacher. In their minds, I always thought uncomfortably, I possessed some sort of secret, some open sesame, which I could divulge if I only would, but which I was wilfully concealing. Some had many things to say but no adequate means of saying them. A few had means to a certain extent but nothing to say. It seemed ironic to me that these talents so rarely met in combination! The fact that each had invested ten dollars in the course was a source of anxiety to me since it was to most of them obviously only an investment.

As I grew more accustomed to night teaching, however, I began to see it in a new light. Not that I ceased to be amused, entertained, and sometimes deeply touched by certain of my students: the taxi-driver who sometimes gave me a free ride home at night and whose fiancée in the telephone exchange had ambition for him; the former trapeze expert in a circus who had a whole menagerie of tales and who longed to share the excitement of his life with the world; the tired little hairdresser who told me once over a cup of coffee that she knew the inner natures of women as no one else could and that she was convinced, if she only persevered, she could learn to write of them. But I began to understand that such eager, vaulting dreams of literary success were actually an end in themselves even though they were doomed to unfulfillment. They were so fervid, I thought, that they must re-create themselves year by year to make household drudgery less monotonous and dull, to lighten days spent in all manner of labor. Each one of my strange assortment of students was living, even as I, not by hair-dressing or shop-keeping or even by preaching and teaching, but by some flaming goal which led us on and on and which we should never reach.

"Life is a pure flame," writes Sir Thomas Browne, "and we live by an invisible sun within us." The mystical import of this truth few of my students could grasp any more than I could grasp it; yet the sun within them and within me was identical with the goal before us. I used to think of this truth as I climbed the steps at eight o'clock of some building at the University or of some public school in St. Paul with people of all ages coming to continue or to begin some study of which they had been deprived in their youth or which was promising them the fulfillment of some long ambition.

It is, in fact, precisely in this nourishment and perpetuation of dreams and visions that I think University Extension work and all other forms of adult education amply justify their existence. The completion of university degrees by attending all manner of classes at night and the training offered to working men in this and that trade or profession are to me neither so important nor so far-reaching in their results as the keeping alive in all sorts of minds desires and devotions which raise life above the level of mere existence. Unless the days of miracles return, few, if any, of my students in Extension classes will ever realize their ambition; yet I trust it has never died within them, for in a sense it is realized by its very presence. And although academic complacency and security are apt to look upon such strivings in the human breast as at best pathetic, I, from four years' experience in night classes, take an opposite view. Life is tolerable, it seems to me, only when some flame burns within one; and if it is kept burning, as I believe it is, in many minds and spirits through the opportunities afforded by University Extension Divisions, then power and glory be unto them from this time forth and even forevermore.

THE COLLEGE OF
ST. CATHERINE

IX

AMONG the blessings of my graduate work at Minnesota were my acquaintance and subsequent friendship with certain nuns belonging to religious communities in Minneapolis and St. Paul. First and chief among these was a middle-aged, vigorous woman known as Sister Lioba, of the Order of St. Joseph of Carondelet. I first met Sister Lioba in our seminar on the eighteenth century novel. She was studying for a master's degree in the hours snatched from her religious duties and from her teaching in the College of St. Catherine, a Roman Catholic college on the outskirts of St. Paul.

Sister Lioba became at once the center and the nucleus of our seminar. This was not because in her black habit and veil, her immaculate white head bands, and wide guimpe she looked different from the others of us or because she represented a way of life foreign to us all; but rather because she at once got more from our reading and contributed more to it than anyone else. Her vow of poverty did not deny her the wealth of Henry

Fielding or her vow of chastity shut her from his distinctly unchaste situations. In fact, the best paper written in our seminar that year was written by Sister Lioba on the humor in *Tom Jones*.

Sister Lioba possessed one of the richest minds I have ever known; and she not only enjoyed it herself but she also shared it with others. She had taken religious vows early in her life, and they had obviously denied her nothing of pleasure but rather increased the depth and the abundance of her nature. She was a tall, rather large woman with blue eyes behind spectacles and a generous, good-humored mouth. She taught English at St. Catherine's; and it was through her that early in our acquaintance I came to know that gracious place and to share in its bounty.

I remember our first journey to St. Catherine's in the street-car one snowy winter afternoon because of an incident which further characterized Sister Lioba and endeared her all the more strongly to me. We were sitting together on the long bench at the end of the car when a little girl got on with her mother and sat opposite us. She became at once engrossed in Sister Lioba's black habit, her white face bands and black veil, her heavy black winter shawl which was well wrapped around her shoulders. After she had gazed with round eyes at what was obviously a strange phenomenon to her, she said to her mother in a high shrill voice:

"Is that a witch?"

Sister Lioba was vastly amused at this question. She leaned across the aisle of the car, quite unconscious of the staring, anxious eyes of all its other passengers, and said to the child:

"No, my dear, I am not a witch, but I have often wished I were."

2

The College of St. Catherine owes its being to the interest and vision of Archbishop Ireland of St. Paul and to the genius of a certain nun, Sister, now Mother, Antonia. Mother Antonia is known throughout the country and beyond it wherever Catholic education is known. Thirty years ago she was the Mary Lyon of the Middle West in her zeal, energy, and vision toward the culture of young women of her faith. There are, indeed, few women in America who have accomplished what she has accomplished for the education of their sex; and when a few years ago the University of Minnesota conferred upon her an honorary degree, there was no person in the vast audience, not even the most immovable of Lutherans, who did not know that she richly deserved it.

As a young nun Sister Antonia had attracted the attention of clergy in diocesan power both by the vividness and strength of her personality and by her talents as a teacher. When Archbishop Ireland early in the nineteen hundreds conceived the

idea of purchasing some high acres above the Mississippi and building thereon a college for Catholic young women, he found in her not only an able
ally and support but a veritable whirlwind of productive activity.

Sister Antonia went at the realization of St.
Catherine's College with everything that she had
in her, and she had literally everything. *Laborare
est orare* was sound doctrine to her. She prayed
while she hustled, and she hustled while she
prayed. The faith within her was justified by her
furious work and her work by her faith. She saw
architects and remade their plans; she sat on stone
heaps and inspired workmen. She laid out grounds
and planted trees. She bought furnishings with
impeccable taste. When the first building of the
new college was completed in 1911 and had opened
its doors to students, she went at another. She
knew every nun in the community and what each
had in her to give to St. Catherine's; and from the
very first she selected her teachers, both regular
and secular, with a judgment that knew no error.

She was herself a woman of fine education. She
had read widely, and seemingly she had forgotten
nothing that she had ever read. She was herself
the best of teachers. She had a positive genius for
detail, and she was a perfectionist in every sense
of the word. Her feverish activity made her not
only apparently omnipresent but completely master of every scene and situation as well. In the

chapel she could be intent upon her own devotions and yet aware of any lack of devotion in her girls. Herself a gracious woman, she instilled graciousness in all about her. Bad manners were sinful to her, and from the start she built up an institution in which politeness was literally never absent. She was a handsome woman with an alert, eager face and a fine carriage. When she swept down the corridors of her college in her black habit on her way to the chapel, or the garden, or the kitchen, or the power-house, everyone upon her swift approach straightened head and shoulders.

I never think of St. Teresa of Avila without seeing Sister Antonia. Both had the same prodigal nature, the same initiative and energy, the same common sense. Both saw in the religious life not only the possibility of beatific visions but the stern necessity for the keeping of one's head. Had Sister Antonia lived in the sixteenth century, she could have forded any number of streams in the Pyrenees and planted any number of religious houses. She could have given, indeed, did give, the same sturdy and wholesome advice to young nuns under her care. There is a story of St. Teresa, familiar, perhaps, yet worth repetition, which has always made me think of Sister Antonia. The Spanish nun was one day riding a sorry mule on one of her numberless journeys through the mountains in the interest of her order when she was

thrown into a rushing stream. While, in anything
but a calm frame of mind, she strove to save herself
from drowning, she heard the voice of God say
to her:

"Murmur not, Teresa. This is the way I treat
my friends."

The saint was quick in reply.

"Small wonder, Lord," said she, "that you have
so few!"

Sister Antonia's type of humor might have
framed precisely this reply; and the simple, direct
relationship with Him to Whom each woman had
given her days and her strength makes the familiarity natural and lovely. After all, one must be
on the best of terms with God to indulge in im-
pertinence at His expense!

3

When I first knew St. Catherine's in 1921, it
consisted of three pleasant buildings on a hill
which sloped to the high bluffs above the Mississippi. Sister Antonia was then planning and praying into being a chapel which from its porch
should command a wide sweep of the western
horizon. This chapel was to be called the Chapel
of Our Lady of Victory, a name which, I thought
with no hint of blasphemy, contained a double significance. I spent an occasional week-end at St.
Catherine's during the two years of my first ac-

quaintance with it through the kind offices of Sister Lioba. I have never known better conversation than went on within its walls in the hours given to conversation. Sister Antonia had high ambition for her nuns, and several of the best teachers among them had studied in Europe, the teacher of psychology at Louvain, the teacher of music in France and Germany. Later the two nuns, who were, with Sister Lioba, to manage the department of English, took honors degrees at Oxford. There was good music at St. Catherine's, and an excellent library. I came to do much of my studying there.

The college when I first knew it contained some two hundred girls. Now there are four times that number. There was also from the beginning a boarding and day school for high-school work. From the first the teaching was excellent and the standards high. Young nuns from the neighboring novitiate completed their college course there; and many of the best students among them went on to Minnesota or to Chicago for advanced degrees.

I was delighted when in the autumn of 1923 Sister Antonia asked me to join her staff as teacher of advanced composition for three hours weekly. I held this post for three years, and I have never enjoyed teaching more in any place. My class was made up of juniors and seniors in college and included both regular and secular dress. We had the best of times together. Two of the nuns in my class, those who were later to study at Oxford, Sister

Antonine and Sister Maris Stella, were of unusual literary ability. The sonnets of the latter I hope are familiar to those who watch the destinies of modern poetry. The former is now dean of St. Catherine's and still teacher of English.

4

But it is not of any possible contribution of my own to St. Catherine's, but of its limitless gifts to me that I wish to write. As time went on, as the Chapel of Our Lady of Victory, modelled on the Cathedral of St. Trophime in Arles, was completed in 1924 and a new science building was erected, I came to know St. Catherine's better from weeks and months spent within the security and seclusion of its high gates. I spent three summers there after I had gone from Minnesota to Smith, returning in 1927 and again in 1928 and 1929. In 1927 I taught in its summer session for Sisters, who came from religious orders elsewhere to study there; in the two latter years I lived at St. Catherine's while I taught at the summer school of the University. I shall always remember those summers of peaceful nights and long, still afternoons.

I asked for and was rewarded by some service expected of me so that I might feel more at home in the convent life. Sometimes I had a room to care for. For two summers the decorating and care of an altar in the chapel were assigned to me. And throughout my stay I was assistant gardener to Sister Alice Irene, who was gardener-in-chief.

Sister Alice Irene was a tall, dark-eyed nun of Swiss extraction, whose profession, aside from religion, was mathematics, and whose mathematics was inseparable from her garden. Like Plutarch she accorded to Plato the saying that God eternally geometrizes; and her chief concern in life, aside from her religion and, indeed, complementing it, was this eternal geometry of God. She taught me far more geometry than I had ever before known by the shapes and the lines of the many flowers which we cultivated and from the shadows cast by the trees at various hours of the day. Our garden at St. Catherine's was flanked by twelve Lombardy poplars, which we named for the twelve apostles, although we accorded the twelfth the name of Matthias, preferring him wisely to Judas Iscariot. The idea, or truth for all that I know, that a spiral begins at zero and ends in infinity was the source of religious veneration to Sister Alice Irene. She thus dealt, like Sir Thomas Browne, in the "mystical mathematicks" of the City of Heaven, seeing all things to begin and to end in order, and then to begin again in that same seemly and comforting fashion.

Sister Alice Irene and I worked for hours on end in the garden of St. Catherine's. She possessed a magical touch with flowers. She had a passion for all things blue: forget-me-nots, love-in-a-mist, bachelor's buttons, blue anchusa, blue morning-glories. She was forever studying seed catalogues to discover what new blue flower was on the market. I always remember her bending above her borders in her black habit, weeding or cultivating or pointing to some theorem in geometry hidden from my sight. She stepped on the earth as though she were a part of it; and she always walked with a fine spring to her feet when she suddenly dropped her tools and hastened across the lawn to the chapel for the examination of her conscience or for one of the daily offices.

I liked the kitchen Sisters at St. Catherine's. Like Brother Laurence they praised the Lord with pots and pans as cymbals and harps and with good food. I used to go into their huge kitchen below the chapel cloister and talk with them as they beat, stirred, and kneaded. The four of them there were ample women of great good humor. They wore large gray aprons over their black habits and usually had a touch of flour somewhere on their black veils. As they bustled about in their convent garb intent upon the means of existence, they somehow connected the religious life with that ageless, and surely religious, necessity of daily bread. One caught in St. Catherine's kitchen that "poetic and moral significance", which Pater discerns in the simplest means of life, once we have torn the veil of triviality and insignificance from them and seen them as they are.

5

Before my association with St. Catherine's I had known nothing whatever of convent life. Had I thought anything about it at all, I should doubtless have concluded from my New England Protestantism, strong within me, that it was a somewhat selfish and cowardly existence undertaken by those who either had no talents with which to face the world or who were, in some odd spiritual way, a bit on the queer side. Nonsensical as is this conception, I have found it held today by the most intelligent of persons. The few nuns I had ever seen had received from me curiosity, possible admiration if their habits became them, and a kind of incredulous pity for the deprivations which they must undergo.

St. Catherine's, from the first time I entered its gates, swept aside all such baseless conceptions as so much outworn baggage. The life there, as in other convents which I have fortunately since known, was far more sane and wholesome than is usual in assemblages of women elsewhere. Every nun, whatever her position in the order, whether she was teaching, studying, cooking, cleaning, or praying, was busy from morning till night. If there were those heart-burnings or regrets, popularly assumed to exist in convents by those who know nothing of them, they were surely not apparent. Doubtless they are no more prevalent in convents than in any other walk of life, since they seem to be the uneasy inheritance of the race in general. Moreover, in convents, unlike much of the world outside them, there is a kind of celestial machinery designed for combating such mental and spiritual disorders.

I have never seen happier people, or funnier for that matter, than the nuns at St. Catherine's. Many of them were Irish by inheritance, some by birth, and their sense of humor was inimitable. I have never known so much laughter elsewhere or such good, rich cause for it. I like the thought, which I learned first at St. Catherine's, that those virtues resulting in sainthood are, first of all, simplicity and joy in the Lord rather than meekness, humility, patience and other less attractive forms of holiness. Knowledge of the saints was not encouraged in my Maine upbringing; but in the years since then I have had a great good time in reading of some of them, and they have added immeasurably to my enjoyment of life.

St. Catherine's, so far as I know, never looked upon me as either a heretic or a heathen. I shared, in so far as my "heresy" allowed me, in its life, from which I gained blessings immeasurable. I liked the peace of its chapel, the quiet of its garden, the friendliness and fun of its nuns, the good manners of its students. I liked the shuffling off of a hundred trivialities, the release of which seemed not only possible but inevitable within its gates. For St. Catherine's believed with Thoreau that one is rich in proportion to the number of things that one can afford to let alone. I liked the long talks with Sister Lioba about all manner of books, of which she knew more than I. I liked our occasional mad games of tennis in which nuns in heavy habits could beat me in a cotton dress to nothing. I liked the single-mindedness at St. Catherine's, the sense that religion was not something to be seized upon in uneasy moments, but natural, like one's hands and feet, and waiting only to be discovered.

6

Through St. Catherine's I came to know other conventual schools and colleges and those who lived therein. In St. Joseph's Academy in St. Paul I made a friend of Mother Seraphine, the sister of Archbishop Ireland. Mother Seraphine was old when I knew her, eighty years and more. She was a great reader and was kind enough to like some of my essays. She had a way of poking me when she was especially excited over something she especially liked before she burst into a gale of laughter. I always thought upon her poke that she was not unlike my grandmother's friends of my childhood with their useful knitting-needles. For she had both tranquillity and breadth of vision like theirs, and, although she had gained hers by other means, the Source of both was one and the same.

I came to know St. Benedict's College near St. Cloud where upon a thousand acres of good Minnesota prairie the Sisters of St. Benedict have their Mother House as well as their college. This Benedictine community is the largest in extent in the country and represents the nearest approximation in modern days to a self-supporting medieval community with its farms and home industries. Two nuns in the English department at St. Benedict's were wonderful teachers, Sister Vivia and Sister Mariella. They brought to their class-rooms a passion alike for literature and for language; and any girls who have studied with them are fortunate.

I like to know that there are places of quiet in a restless world where even a descendant of the New England Puritans is made to feel at home.

I went back to St. Catherine's a few months ago. The daffodils were in bloom in the garden beneath the shadow of the Twelve Apostles although Sister Alice Irene no longer tends them. She is now Mother Superior of St. Margaret's Academy in Minneapolis. Mother Antonia still lends her strength and her wisdom to the college which she and God have made.

The two sounds which always bring St. Catherine's back to me were still there: the silence, which there is sound, and the quick, subdued, diligent tread of many footsteps moving always hither and yon upon the Lord's business. They always have made me think of these footsteps upon the mountains in Isaiah, bringing good tidings and publishing peace.

Sister Lioba died a few weeks after my visit, full of years and of countless good times, spent both with God and with His many diverse children. She told me once while we were both in the graduate school that she hoped it would be permitted her in the next world to meet Henry Fielding since she wanted to thank him for *Joseph Andrews* and *Tom Jones*. I trust, as much for his sake as for hers, that they have met in some pleasant roadside inn, full of life and bustle, and with Parson Adams by the fire with his Aeschylus. For no one more than Sister Lioba ever has believed the good Parson's contention that life is only to be learned from books.

Chapter X

MY EXPERIENCE AS A
LECTURER

X

I HAVE never been able to determine to my own satisfaction the status or the function of those who, for one reason or another, address from time to time various groups of the American public. A lecturer is, I assume, something of a teacher, although I have often thought the role of preaching and not infrequently of acting included in his diverse offerings. At all events, since speaking upon many and varied occasions has come to be part of my life as a teacher, I am impelled, in order to make the story of my teaching complete, to record certain of the compensations of the lecturing profession, if profession it is.

I began my experience as a lecturer at the University of Minnesota and for no other reason than the occasional modest remuneration which it afforded me. Almost immediately, however, I added to the monetary remuneration the chance of finding myself in all manner of odd situations, which were never without interest to me and which often added to my pleasant stock of notions about life in general and human beings in particular.

A large section of the American public is unique in that it is more willing to be talked to than any other people under the sun. Whether this characteristic has its source in an honest desire for self-improvement (for lecturers are popularly assumed to deal in self-improvement), in superfluous energy, or in a kind of mental lethargy, I have never been able to discover. But whatever its source the American avidness to listen to someone on all manner of topics, even to me, has added immeasurably to my pleasure in life.

In my earliest days as a lecturer I had the good companionship of the present Dean of Smith College, who was then an instructor in English at the University of Minnesota. When occasional requests came from certain women's clubs in Minneapolis or St. Paul, or in their near vicinity, for lectures at ten dollars each, Miss Nicolson and I decided between ourselves which was the less ill-fitted to earn the ten dollars. One day, I remember, requests came simultaneously from two groups of women, one of which wished to be enlightened on Job and the other on Dante. Since neither of us knew too much about either of these philosophers and poets, we tossed a coin, Job falling to me, Dante to her. Then we repaired immediately to the University library in order to learn enough about our respective subjects to be worth ten dollars each.

When high-school commencements began in June, we departed to various Minnesota towns to uplift the young. For such addresses in the early years of the nineteen-hundreds we received a slightly larger compensation. Thirty-five dollars was the maximum in cash, but a bonus in humorous experience was often added to this sum. We marched with graduating classes into town halls on blistering evenings, decked out with class ribbons and surrounded by much curiosity, not to say veneration, from both parents and youth. What we had to say was without doubt paltry enough; but we learned to say it with a weather eye out to note whether or not it was "taking"; whether a swift change in subject matter or in method of approach was imperative. To earn our thirty-five dollars we slept in all manner of homes, ate all manner of foods, and listened to parlor duets and recitations by all manner of children. We cautioned parents in private upon the upbringing of their children and in private advised boys and girls as to their futures; we met local celebrities, inspected town parks and cemeteries, admired all manner of babies and sometimes cared for them while their mothers were preparing supper. In short, we learned early in our experience that the mere giving of a lecture is the least requirement made of lecturers or even expected of them.

2

I am informed that there is a society in a certain Middle Western university called *The Society for the Prevention of Cruelty to Lecturers.* This society has its corresponding secretary who writes to the imminent lecturer in advance to ascertain whether or not he wishes to be given a dinner or a luncheon before his lecture, whether he prefers a hotel, even at his own expense, to the guest room of an American home, whether or not he is interested in local or college libraries, in gymnasiums, amusement parks, new dormitories, war memorials, town halls, and churches; in short, whether he wishes to be "entertained" or left severely alone. Lecturers being what they often are, such a society might well have its counterpart in all our colleges and in connection with all those multifarious organizations which specialize in lectures and lecturers. The society might well, indeed, bear a double title; for I know far too well the heavy toll which lecturers often exact from those who engage them, meet them, care for them, bear with them, and finally listen to what they have to say.

Certain lecturers are volubly fussy about lights, microphones, acoustics, platforms, hotel rooms, and even weather. Some wish to be well fed before they speak; others abhor the very mention of food. Some must go into the silence before they mount the platform; others are greatly stimulated by a cocktail. Certain women lecturers have a way of postponing shopping and hair-dressing until they reach the town in which they are to lecture, whereupon they desire counsel and companionship. I know one well-known lecturer who charges extra if he is forced to dine with certain of his audience before he begins to inform and uplift. I know another who some years ago threw an entire town into confusion by insisting that the chiming of a clock be stopped during her speech. Since this clock had chimed for many years and since there was a community sentiment, even tradition, about its never-ceasing voice, the command of the lecturer proved costly in the extreme.

Lecturers often talk together of the punishments which they undergo during an extended lecture tour; yet I must acknowledge that punishments have been in my experience far fewer than compensations. Sometimes, indeed, seeming punishments have been transformed into unexpected rewards. I confess to an enjoyment of unfamiliar towns and cities, to a certain pleasure in the pride of their inhabitants, to an interest in all sorts of human beings whom I shall probably never see again but whose friendliness toward me is memorable. I have been taken to see a waterfall in Utah by some charming Mormons who were quite willing to supplement the waterfall by stories, requested by me, of their Mormon upbringing. I have inspected Oklahoma oil-fields for the first time under the supervision of the most humorous of women of whom I shall always think with gratitude. I have seen the fine chapel of the University of Pittsburgh in the company of a nameless young man whose face I have forgotten but whose knowledge of stained glass far exceeded my own. I have been taken at midnight on my own tired feet to see the treasures in the Wrenn library at the University of Texas and forgotten my weariness in the pride of my conductors.

Surely the compensations of the lecturer lie far afield from his lecturing. I have sat in sackcloth and ashes for too many hours in too many hotel rooms over what I have failed to say or over what I have stupidly said to look upon my speeches as any compensation or pleasure in themselves. Surely I do not lecture for any infrequent glow of satisfaction from my own words! Nor do the checks in payment for my services, although now they are somewhat larger than ten and thirty-five dollars, represent to me the real reason why I still board trains bound toward various parts of the United States. Nor does any notion of bettering the public, of "purifying the national taste", in Cardinal Newman's words, lead me to pack my suitcases. In fact, no mere monetary or even altruistic urge could induce me thus to inconvenience myself or to interrupt the satisfying orderliness of my days.

I continue to give lectures here and there for only one reason, a reason identical with that which moves nine-tenths of the human race toward any sort of action: *I like to do so.* I enjoy such peregrinations, such fleeting, chance acquaintanceships, in spite of many sad moments over the character of my public addresses. *Omne ignotum pro magnifico est,* writes Tacitus: "The unknown is always fascinating." And it is precisely this truth, and this alone, which leads me to leave my pleasant home now and then for parts and people unknown.

A train intrigues me. Day coach, streamliner, lower berth, parlor car, or compartment, each is always new to me. I like settling my belongings, putting my hat in a paper bag, drinking a cocacola in the club-car before bedtime, arranging my pillows to read at night. I like the assurance that no one knows me or wants to, that no one can call me to the telephone, that I am cleanly cut off in space from a hundred annoying responsibilities. I like the impersonality of trains, the fact that I am alone, the knowledge that interest, concern, disapproval, enmity, even affection, are somewhere far behind me, that I am enclosed in my own small space, and that this distinct physical boundary can free my mind as nothing else can.

In the past few years I have done most of my reading on trains. Even newspapers, which I commonly hate, are welcome there. I buy local papers to learn the social news of Omaha or Fort Worth or Salt Lake City. People create themselves before my eyes at their weddings or engagement parties. Jane Austen is my best companion on most of my journeyings. Mr. Woodhouse and his diet, Mrs. Bennet, Mrs. Jennings, Mr. Darcy, Henry Tilney, and Anne Eliot are always at their best somewhere in the pleasant monotony of the Middle Western plains. Dickens, too, flourishes on trains, Trollope, Fielding, and Charlotte Brontë, though never Emily.

Although I am rarely loquacious on trains, I am often vastly entertained by the conversations of others. Once while I journeyed from St. Paul to Duluth two stout women in chairs opposite my own talked for three hours on the nature of virtue, a truly Platonic subject, if delivered without the wisdom of Socrates in the *Protagoras*. One of these women, who ate innumerable caramels as she talked, was as barren as the Sophist himself and a sore trial to her companion. Ever since that afternoon caramels have borne an odd moral significance to me, so that, fond as I am of them, I am never quite light-hearted in their consumption.

Not infrequently the porter on my car is a person as well. Two years ago when I crossed the country in January, my porter, who was always humming gospel tunes as he worked, discovered from the conductor, who was much intrigued by the length of my ticket, that I was on a lecture tour. Just before we reached Seattle, he surprised me by asking if I perchance spoke about the Lord in my lectures. I told him with some apology that I feared I did not, that I instead spoke only about books.

"Well," said he, "I don't quite see, ma'am, how you can miss talking about the Lord. He wrote the only good book."

I am always excited when I draw near my destination, especially if I have never been there before. The renewal of acquaintanceships, pleasant though it may be, is never quite so exhilarating as the first meeting with the unknown. I wonder what manner of man or woman will meet me and what my hotel room will be like. The thoughts of a bath and the straightening out of my possessions are excitements in themselves. I wonder if among the unknown persons whom I am to meet someone among them will "click" with me, to become henceforth a permanent possession rather than a memory, although perhaps never to be seen again.

Scattered here and there over the country are odd, bright spots which stand for moments of swift understanding between me and those heretofore strangers. When I perchance see a map of the United States, there are upon it these tiny gleams of light encircling the dots which are certain cities and towns. A city in Texas glows with such light, for there I met a woman whom I shall never forget. She told me when she came to my hotel to see me that she was very deaf. She said this quite simply, even humorously, and later she let me into her secret. She said that she had been deaf for years and that she had come to know deafness as her greatest of blessings because of one awful day when she had heard *everything*. A specialist on the morning of that fateful day had fitted her with some wonderful mechanism, and, for twelve hours, she had heard all manner of things: the gossip of her friends, a disconcerting lecture, the babble of a tea-party, the advertisements over the radio, and many opinions of many persons upon many subjects. She said it was the worst day of her life. At night she returned the illuminating mechanism to the specialist and since then has been surrounded by complete security and contentment.

There is an ugly town in Indiana which I should dislike were it not for a chance acquaintance there, whom I met on a dull and dirty street, and who had nothing at all to do with my coming to lecture. I was out for a solitary walk and engaged at the moment in wondering what sort of audience such a town could provide when I was startled by a hand placed upon my arm. I turned quickly to meet the eyes of a small and very old woman. She was, however, not at all interested in me as a person but only in my feet, which were clad in some stout English shoes. She apologized for accosting me. She had followed me for two blocks, she said, once she had seen my feet. She suffered from constant pain in her own, and my shoes had so impressed her with the possibility of relief that she had ventured to ask me where I had procured them. I have rarely felt so cruel upon any occasion in my life as when I told her that they had been made in London.

"In London, dear?" she said. "Imagine that. Well, I suppose I must get on with my pain."

The swift changes of weather on my winter journeyings always interest me. I make it a habit to get out of the train at stations where we stop in order to detect the temperature. I like to go to bed in the cold dampness of Chicago and wake to peach trees in the sun. I love an afternoon of driving rain, a morning of falling snow, a night of intense cold. Once in North Dakota when we were delayed through waiting for a late freight train, I walked a mile upon the prairie in cold ten degrees below zero. Orion was brighter then than I have ever seen him, Taurus, Aldebaran, and Sirius.

3

Of all the forty-eight states in the Union, and I have been in practically all of them, I think I have enjoyed Ohio most. Perhaps my assurance arises from the fact that so many people in Ohio have been friendly to me, that I know so many kind towns and cities set upon its flat plains or among its gentle hills. Perhaps of all Middle

Western states Ohio retains more of New England and, therefore, more of home to me. At all events I have come to the conclusion that Ohio will forevermore for me hold something rare and fine. I have travelled in Ohio, east, west, north, and south, at all seasons of the year. I have baked in its hot June suns and shivered in its late autumn cold. I have watched its snow fall while journeying in a bus from Toledo to Lima and seen through the white obscurity the red and purple shadows of its winter oaks in the hollows of its hills. I have been to Delaware in the spring when the daffodils were in bloom and cardinals whistling in the back yard of a house where strangers at once made me feel a member of their home. I have been to Cleveland and Toledo, Columbus and Delaware, Lima, Cincinnati, and Canton, with its eager, friendly people, and to the lovely town of Springfield.

Among others of its virtues Ohio is the one state in the Union which has given me neither a chicken patty nor vanilla ice-cream with chocolate sauce to eat. As all lecturers know, a chicken patty is the *pièce de résistance* of most meals accorded them, and the patty is almost invariably followed by a mis-named chocolate sundae. I am still fond of a chicken patty in spite of endless repetition; but the intuition or the forethought of Ohio in avoiding it places that pleasant state in a realm apart. Instead of chicken patties I have had the most delectable of foods in Ohio. Not even Kansas City where I have been sumptuously fed or Santa Barbara where I once ate a memorable lunch out-of-doors in bright January sunshine can equal the towns of Ohio in their food. I have always looked upon cooking as one of the major arts; and Springfield, Ohio, has an inimitable art colony of cooks. I came home from Springfield filled with rare viands and with so many recipes in my mind and on paper that a by-word in my house has been *Springfield* ever since my sojourn there.

There was great good fun in Springfield as well as good food. My audience there took neither itself nor me too seriously, a state of mind which all lecturers hope for and too seldom find.

4

Yet I think the greatest gift which my going across the country has given me is the sudden sight from train windows of things unfamiliar and, therefore, of extra enchantment, their very suddenness increasing the profundity of their effect. I have all sorts of these swift glimpses, these benisons of time and place, in my memory, to be taken out and looked at again and again whenever I feel the need of them. Sometimes without waiting for my summoning they flash out from my subconscious mind, re-creating themselves upon all manner of odd and unrelated occasions.

I woke once early in the morning at an ugly

town in Iowa, called curiously enough Arcadia. It was New Year's day, I remember. The long, wide fields were ploughed; the soil was like the richest of black velvet. The sun just rising sent a burst of light, as I watched, over the blackness of the land so that the velvet took on a sumptuous glow and increased its impression of wealth and depth. I did not wonder at the name of the town when I had once seen its surrounding fields in this engulfing light. Perhaps, I thought, it had been named some morning at sunrise after its first ploughing.

Once in the Far West, in Utah or, perhaps, in Nevada, I travelled through a snowstorm in the late afternoon. The gray, desert land was covered with sagebrush upon which the snow had clustered in such a way that the undulating clumps of brush were identical with waves of the sea. Groups of cattle here and there rose from the obscurity of the snow for all the world like the dim outlines of ships; and the misty indistinct horizon held all the illimitableness of the ocean.

I went north from Sacramento one winter day in the most brilliant sunshine I have ever seen. In the seemingly near distance beyond the green fields Mt. Shasta, white with unbroken snow, rose into the bluest of skies. Now and then over the greenness of the land a white heron stalked or flew; and suddenly one, not white but as blue as the sky above, rose from the green earth, the sun on its plumage making it an aquamarine of light.

I have seen from train windows the long line of the Pacific breaking upon yellow beaches below gaunt, threadbare hills of rock with gulls swooping and circling above their summits; oranges hanging on small, shining, compact trees; a field of scarlet poinsettias. Once I went through the High Sierras on a bright morning when the tall black spruces sent shadows of purple across ravines filled with snow. Once in Maine at low tide I watched the wind sweeping over marsh grasses and knew suddenly that, for some odd and unaccountable reason, it was the saddest and most solitary act of Nature.

These things and others like them make me take exception to the words of Ovid: "There is nothing in the whole world which abides." *Nihil est toto quod perstet in orbe.* Rather I say with Virgil: *Haec olim meminisse juvabit.* "I shall take pleasure in remembering these things hereafter."

It is for these that I pack my suit-cases, endure tired feet and the memory of my own ill-begotten words, eat too generously of chicken patties, and return home dirty and tired. For I am among those who glory in the possession of a country which, from ocean to ocean, holds within itself so many sure and certain glimpses of eternal life.

THE TEACHING OF ENGLISH

XI

MY GRANDMOTHER, who died at eighty-seven, was as she grew older more and more perplexed over the meaning and significance of my profession in life. Whenever I returned home for summer vacations, she always cornered me and asked exactly what the teaching of English meant. Since no such pedagogical term was used in her day and generation, she added to her bewilderment a kind of uneasy suspicion lest this strange subject to which I gave my time and strength was in some way inferior to those more obvious subjects such as Latin or mathematics. Upon each return we used to have disturbing colloquies of this nature:

"Just what do you do when you teach English? Do you mean that you teach your students to read?"

"Yes, and a great many more things."

"What things?"

"Well, I try to teach them to write as well as to read."

"What do you mean—to write?"

"To say what they think in good English."

"Do you mean *grammar?*"

"Yes, partly. But there is a lot more to it than grammar."

"What, exactly?"

"Well, I try to teach them to write good sentences that mean something."

"Do you mean you teach them to be writers?"

"No. I can't teach them to be writers. But I try to teach them to say what they think."

"Do people nowadays have to be taught to say what they think?"

"Yes, and they have to be taught to think straight."

"To think straight about what?"

"Well, about the things they do think about, and the things they read."

"What things do they read?"

"Oh, poetry and essays and novels."

"Can't they read those things by themselves?"

"Well, I try to show them what poetry and prose mean, not just what they say in so many words."

"You mean you read things like Shakespeare and Dickens in your classes?"

"Yes, and many other things, too."

"It can't be so hard just to read things and talk about them as to teach, say, Latin or arithmetic, is it?"

"Yes. I think it's a great deal harder."

"Well, maybe. But it doesn't seem so to me. . . . Do you like teaching English?"

"Yes, I like it better than anything else in the world."

After such a conversation as this with my grandmother I always felt a kind of odd insecurity assailing me. I wondered if the teaching of English was as vague an exercise and occupation as my own answers to her questions. I felt, in fact, sure only about two of my answers: first, that the teaching of English is at once the hardest teaching in the world to do and, second, that it is more fun to do than anything else in the world.

2

After twenty-two years spent in the teaching of college English I still believe true the first of my contentions to my puzzled grandmother: that English is the most difficult of all subjects to teach. Unlike others more tidy because more clearly defined, English has no *terminus ab quo,* no *terminus ad quem.* More closely related to life than any other study, even than the sciences, it embraces literally everything within its invisible and illimitable boundaries. And yet, on the other hand, in itself it baffles definition. It is a language, yet, because of the very necessity of its use, it lacks in most imaginations the dignity and the charm of an ancient or even of a modern foreign tongue. It is an art, yet again the familiar and the necessary, the daily and the commonplace, dim its aesthetic qualities and possibilities. It seems the hand-maiden to other subjects rather than the mistress of them all, simply because no other subject can be understood without it. Thus the teacher of English is hampered at the start by misconceptions so natural and inevitable that they are doubly hard to put to rout.

Of all the excellent teachers of college English whom I have known I have never discovered one who knew precisely what he was doing. Therein have lain their power and their charm. I have come, indeed, to think that a firm hold upon definite objectives and methods by the teacher of English is likely to mark him as mediocre or even as poor at his job. Our objectives are as nebulous and intangible as are our methods, for the simple reason that we are dependent for the efficacy of both upon the multifarious imaginations of our students. The success of our teaching like the nature of it is forevermore conditioned by the capacities of the minds with which we work, by the wealth or poverty of perception, by the presence or absence of humor, by the possession or lack of understanding and vision. The meaning and value of any piece of literature are rarely the same to any two persons; the arrangement of words in a sentence may mean everything, something, or nothing both to those who read them and to those who labor to write them. *Man proposes, but God disposes* is a truth to be learned as quickly as possible by all teachers of English! And it is through the extreme flexibility of his mind, through the recognition that he is but a variable means to a most variable end, that the teacher of English reaps his variable reward.

Once at Hillside I was endeavoring to teach a stupid and somewhat sullen boy of thirteen the fundamentals of English grammar. We were dealing one morning with adverbs of manner, those sprightly parts of speech which add life and action to their verbs. Seeing the necessity for extreme simplicity in my explanations, I made the insecure announcement that most adverbs of manner end in *ly*. I wrote various of these on the blackboard: quick*ly*, slow*ly*, gent*ly*, noisi*ly*, smooth*ly*, stern*ly*, silent*ly*. Then I turned to the boy and said:

"I want you to think quietly for a few minutes and then give me some adverbs of manner of your own."

"I don't need to think," he said instantly. *"July."*

Since that day I have had many such doors so summarily slammed upon my objectives that I have learned to look upon them merely as my own loosely defined and pleasant possessions, which may never become, indeed, often *can* never become, the property of those whom I teach. I have learned that for one student who sees reality and excitement in an adverb, there are many who will never see a part of speech other than a part of speech. I have learned that for one student who comes to college with a sense of the dignity and the delicacy in words, there are many, even from the best of schools, to whom the writing of English is stupid and useless and the careful and thoughtful reading of it only a bit less so. I have learned that my methods must be as different and varied as the different and varied personalities of my students, who from the start are governed by forces over which I have small control. I have learned that to know precisely what I am doing in any given class at any given moment is a state of mind as intolerably dull for my students as for myself and as arid as the proverbial Valley of Baca.

It is, then, this very necessity for elasticity of mind on the part of the teacher, for quick and intelligent changes in approach, which makes the teaching of English such a difficult job. We deal with the most personal and most fortified of possessions, with thoughts and feelings, suggestions and impressions, notions, fancies, predilections, ideas. We learn, if we are any good at our work, to welcome opposition, opinions different from our own, heresies, heterodoxies, iconoclasms. Our delight lies in the activity of awakened minds to any end at all. For we deal not with ends but with means. If Karl Marx dictates the criticism of certain of our students, we keep our heads; if James Joyce rather than Wordsworth proves the bread of life to others, we rejoice in this form of nourishment, strange though it may be to us; if Pater's style stirs someone to rebellion, we turn to Hem-

ingway until the rebellion is quelled, if it ever is.
We learn that we can be firm toward our own loy-
alties and yet not immovable toward others. Our
one aim is to intensify the powers of thinking and
of feeling in those whom we teach; and the only
method we have of doing this is to open, through
countless ways, every possible avenue to thought,
emotion, and expression and to keep ourselves alive
while we are doing so.

3

I feel sure that all honest teachers of English
admit from the start that their job, difficult as it
may be, is, first of all, a self-indulgence. For I still
believe true the second of my contentions to my
grandmother that the teaching of English is more
fun to do than anything else in the world. The best
of us have come into the profession because we
have been unable to keep out of it. In one way or
another we fell in love with books early in life,
with their words and phrases, their music and
rhythm, their people and their events, their meaning and their thought; and to attempt to convey
to others our own passion has been the simplest
means open to us of continuing therein ourselves.

Most college professors of English like, as
they reach what is known as the "top", to stick
to their own fields of study and enthusiasm. This
becomes their own particular form of self-indul-

gence. If they are mad about Chaucer or Shakespeare or the Seventeenth Century, they like to teach within their own boundaries. They are not eager to meet the incoming hordes of college freshmen, who, for better or for worse, write themes which must be read, and read badly the books assigned to them. They prefer to deal with students who have gone through the mill of Freshman English and who have, presumably, come out refined and ready for more delicate and costly nourishment. But, unlike the majority, I am one who, even after twenty-two years of trying to teach English to freshmen, still find its ways ways of pleasantness if not always paths of peace.

Too many young teachers of freshmen bring an unfortunate residue of the graduate schools into their class-rooms. Coming into college teaching fresh (or perhaps not so fresh) from the doctorate, they need some time, at the expense of their students, to realize that a fund of knowledge is the worst possible capital with which to begin their work and that the emulation of their graduate professors is the worst possible way to teach freshmen. In this teaching, resiliency and humor, liveliness and enthusiasm, informality and companionship, count for far more than knowledge. I have found from long experience that the teacher of freshmen who has had past experience in secondary schools is far more likely to succeed in college teaching, with or without the doctorate, than one who has gone directly from the bachelor's degree to further study.

I have spent some of the most pleasant hours of my life with college freshmen. I have found that succeeding years do not much alter the crop in spite of increasingly excellent teaching in many of the schools. Perhaps the average seventeen- or eighteen-year-old mind is subject to certain well-defined boundaries, which await for their extension the freedom and independence of college. At all events, with relatively few exceptions, my freshmen exhibit the same mental habits and characteristics, different as they are in temperament and personality. To many of them the use of words is a tolerable exercise but often quite unconnected with thought. It is fun to snap them out of sloppy thinking or to bring them up sharply from the abyss of no thinking at all; to make them conscious of the interdependence of words and thoughts; to make them see that a paragraph is a logical procession of sentences and thoughts which march along together, each depending upon the other; to make them see words with their eyes; to teach them that ears alone are the most dangerous of senses.

It is, indeed, this dependence upon ears, this multiplying of words without knowledge, this *inanis verborum torrens* scorned by Quintilian, which, to me, forms the first task of the teacher of Freshman English. This it is, as we all know, which lends to the reading of early themes the zest of a treasure-hunt. Even in Smith College, where entering students have been exceptionally well trained in the best of schools, this dependence upon hearing alone can give birth to such a sentence as this which recently began a freshman theme:

I have long since refused to accept those age-old traditions of life, death, and God.

Or to this moving bit of portraiture:

Over the mantel hung a portrait of my grandfather. He had never married, never loved, and never deviated from the paths of respectability.

The writing of English has, I believe, never been sufficiently respected as a means to mental discipline; yet surely the power to visualize as well as to hear the words which one places upon paper is the first "objective" of the teacher. To use English fluently and well can never be taught. All writing, says Emerson in one of his essays, comes by the Grace of God, a truth recognized early by all wise teachers of freshmen. But straight thinking, even although it is destined to remain within narrow limits, can be taught by patience, energy, and humor; and this training in the careful, rather than the skillful, use of words seems to me the chief reason for the continued existence of English composition in our colleges.

I like to teach my freshmen to read, and I have

ample opportunity to do so since at least fifty percent of them come to college without really knowing how. They are not, of course, so bad at narrative or even at certain forms of poetry, but an essay leaves them wandering in labyrinthine mazes. The meaning of what they read is lost in a succession of words; the personality of single words means little if anything. I understand that there are now specialists in the exercise of reading whose business it is to remedy defects by all sorts of tests and methods. My own manner of remedy will doubtless seem unsound to them; yet it has not been without effect. I like to teach my students to see a word in terms of light and color, whether it is clear and shining, heavy and dark, black or white or yellow; to show them that any page of any given book has a character of its own through mere letters even before the words themselves are seen as words. I have discovered in my own teaching that once single words are grasped in their appearance, their sound, their meaning, and in the countless suggestions and associations which each holds within itself, the power to read more difficult prose comes as though by magic.

I have found that the most minute detail sometimes stirs the imagination. I have always been sensitive to the drama in punctuation although to most of my students the mastery of its use is drudgery and its existence at best only a matter of convenience. I like to convince them that in itself it is

an art and that the skillful employment of it, as
Charles Lamb so well knew, can add personality
and suggestion to their themes. I like to awaken
them to the vivacity of a comma, the dignity and
silence of a semi-colon, the suspense and quicken-
ing latent in a question mark, the redundancy and
danger in an exclamation point.

I have always felt sorry that figures of speech,
which used to be taught thirty years ago when the
science of Rhetoric was still in good and honorable estate, have now become honorable points of
ignorance to many teachers and matters of inattention to most students. I still find similes the
most provoking of subjects for study and appreciation. My freshmen and I take delight in them
and in the imagination which prompts them. I
like to try to show what is behind the desire, instinctive in us all, to compare one thing with another; how comparisons arise from one's background, nature, and experience; how the range and
wealth of imagination differ in the individual. I
like to show how a simile gives a double picture,
how it at the same time heightens, clarifies, and
intensifies one's feeling, thought, or image.

*As the mountains are roundabout Jerusalem, so
the Lord is roundabout His people, henceforth and
even forever.*

*The mail-coach it was that distributed over the
face of the land, like the opening of apocalyptic*

*vials, the heart-shaking news of Trafalgar, of Sala-
manca, of Vittoria, of Waterloo.*

We go on a still hunt for similes in my class in
anything which we happen to be reading. Sometimes I am sufficiently mad or sanguine to pro-
pose that we try our minds and hands at them.
One of my freshmen, whom God disposed of early,
writes:

*The sun was sinking below the western horizon
like a new penny dropped into a slot machine in
order to bring out the night.*

Another, through whom He is still working,
says:

*When I was very young, the fields stretching
on and on before our farmhouse door meant nothing to me but land; when I was happy, as a place
to play upon, when I was sad, as a place where no
one ever came. Now as I look upon them they are
wide and long like the thoughts of quiet people,
like the wish to know more and more of things that
cannot be seen.*

The first makes me wholesomely conscious of
the limitations imposed upon all teachers of English composition; the second makes me want to
stick to my job if only for my own sake.

Now that terms as terms have passed from class
vocabularies, now that *unity, coherence,* and *emphasis* have gone, never, we hope, to return, now

that mere text-books have lost their old significance and become uneasy means to a questionable end, the teacher of English becomes not so much a task-master as the companion of his students. What we are after is an awakened consciousness, differing in each individual, an excitement in thinking, reading, and writing for their own sake, new discoveries, new enthusiasms, the casting off, or the retention with better understanding, of the old. What we want is to stimulate the love of mental adventure and of constructive doubt, to create emotional satisfaction in the things of the mind, to reveal through books the variety and the wonder of human experience.

How we do these things matters not at all. The numberless ways of their accomplishment reside in the numberless personalities of those of us who teach. The one thing that does matter is that we shall be awake and alive, alert and eager, flexible and unperturbed, likable and exciting. Once we are these things, we can cast away all the aphorisms and methods conceived and issued by the teachers' colleges as so much useless baggage, for we are vastly better off without them.

4

Like all teachers of English I indulge myself by communicating to my students my own enthusiasms in literature. Perhaps this practice is after

all not so much a self-indulgence as it is a necessity;
for no teacher is at his best in dealing with something which does not satisfy himself. My freshmen
each year read a Greek play with me simply because *Medea* or *The Trojan Women, Electra* or
The Trachiniae have delighted and nourished me
through many years. To most of them new doors
are opened; to the few who never enter in, Euripides and Sophocles, even in a good translation,
surely need make no apology to college freshmen!
From the ancients we move to the moderns to
realize that art has no boundaries in time or in
space. One of my students discovered last year that
Homer in the *Odyssey* and Willa Cather in *My
Antonia* held ideas as well as principles of literature in common, a discovery which for her and
for us all brought the old and the new suddenly
together.

I have found this companionship in literature
very much the same whether I share it with freshmen or with my older college students, who study
with me the fiction of the eighteenth and nineteenth
centuries. With both, my desires are the same. I
want to make both see that mere pleasurable excitement in any given piece of literature is not a
sufficient end in itself but rather a spring-board
toward something better than itself. I want to
make both conscious of the manifold ways by
which an author has caused this pleasurable excitement, to make both understand how the prod-

uct of an artist's mind can be made even more
beautiful in the light of a reader's intelligence. I
want to make both realize that all art is thus cre-
ative, that one mind creates in another perhaps
even a greater abundance than was in its own, and
that in this sense the reader becomes an artist together with the writer.

The analysis of books which is necessary in order to gain this understanding is irksome to some
students, since the taste of many readers, in college
and out, is but a vague sense of likes and dislikes
from which they do not wish to be dislodged. And
yet a standard of literary appreciation is the one
aim of the teacher of literature, for from its sure
foundation a critical sense is added to the mere enjoyment of reading. The vision of the artist can
never be re-created in the reader without a knowledge of his work, his ways and means; and this
knowledge is dependent upon seeing the whole
only through the sum of all its parts.

I have found analysis to be the most exciting of
literary occupations; and I hope I have managed
to convey a measure of excitement to those who
break down and rebuild with me. The sharpened
powers which analysis gives extend far beyond the
novel or poem analyzed. Not only is the whole
seen in all its truth, but the parts take on each its
own value. The words and sentences, motifs and
music, images and figures, characters and situ-

ations, a memorable phrase, lines of description or of thought—each exists for itself as well as for the whole; and each in the mind of the reader becomes linked with numberless suggestions and associations from out his own experience. The analysis of novels turns mere events into ideas, which, according to Santayana, is the function of literature; the analysis of poems transfigures words into emotion; the analysis of essays gives form and body to ideas and reflections.

There is a figure in a fragment of Sappho, which, regardless of the unknown thought of the poet, always suggests to me this necessity of breaking up a whole in order to endow it with the breath of life.

Like the hyacinth which the shepherd tramples underfoot upon the mountain, but which yet blooms purple on the ground.

"The literature that is of lasting value is an accident," writes a recent essayist. "It is something that happens to one." It is this accident, this sudden happening in the minds of our students, which is our goal as teachers of literature whatever our "methods" may be. It is this accident which turns readers into artists through their sudden understanding that the values of art and life are one and the same. It is this accident for which we work and wait, knowing always that the capacity for intelligent appreciation of literature among a people means far more to the life of that people than any works of art it may produce.

5

I have often wondered whether my grandmother's mind in some future state has been clarified as to what the teaching of English really means. My own remains as delightfully vague as my answers to her questions many years ago or as this incomplete and uncertain description of my pleasant days with students. And since any immortality which there may be may find no room for books or even for enlightenment upon their richest use, I seize upon the nearer immortality granted to those whose life is in literature, knowing that this life, too, in the words of Ovid is identical with the power of his heaven, *Immensa est finemque non habet.*

Chapter XII

SMITH COLLEGE

XII

I CAME to Smith College in the autumn of 1926. Like most New Englanders I had for years planned upon returning to my own part of the country, like most New Englanders felt always that, in spite of my enjoyment of the Middle West, I was only sojourning there. This desire to return home for the remainder of my life as a teacher was strengthened by the recognition of the attitude of the universities toward the promotion of women to the higher ranks of practically all departments. Generous as the University of Minnesota had been toward me, I was forced to acknowledge that a full or even an associate professorship in English would probably be denied me on the ground of my sex. The women's colleges, I knew, raised no such barriers to a decent ambition to reach the top of one's profession, in name at least; and I possessed, I think naturally enough, the desire to complete my experience in a position which should not only permit me to teach in my chosen field of English literature but which should also allow me to feel that I had reached the goal set for myself by myself.

Of all the women's colleges, I had in my mind chosen Smith as the one most alluring to me. There was, without doubt, a good deal of sentiment in my choice. Since that glowing day when I had set forth through the tumbling Berkshire hills to seek my fortune in the Middle West, I had looked upon that portion of New England as holding more than a little of me. Whenever upon my returns home I reached the town of Pittsfield, I had felt a kind of tenacious satisfaction enfolding me. I had always been ill at ease in cities or even in large towns. I knew that I wanted to spend the rest of my life as a teacher in the country, and I could think of no country more satisfying than that holding the high orchards, the streams, and the hills of Western Massachusetts.

There was, however, another and still stronger urge toward Smith College. I had known for years of President Neilson, read his books, loved his interpretation of English poetry, heard him lecture in Minneapolis. I knew something of the respect and admiration in which he was held by certain members of his faculty known to me and, almost of more importance, by many of the students at Smith. The impression which I had gained of him had been substantiated and deepened by several of my professors in the graduate school who had studied under him at Harvard. Cecil

Moore, of whom I have already written in my chapter on the University of Minnesota, told me one day of a cartoon which had appeared in the Harvard *Lampoon*. Beneath a drawing of Mr. Neilson, sitting with a volume of *Paradise Lost* in his hands, was written:

> "Milton! Thou shouldst be living at this hour:
> Neilson is reading thee."

Knowing full well those qualities in teachers which construct and establish the attitude of their students toward them, I saw in Mr. Moore's reminiscence only added proof that I should like to teach under William Allan Neilson if only he could be brought to smile upon my desire.

His smile came in January, 1926, through the kind offices of a trustee of Smith College, Miss Marguerite Wells of Minneapolis. His letter offered me an associate professorship at Smith, the opportunity to teach in my own field of English studies, and the suggestion that there might be advancement in rank should I prove worthy of it. I accepted his offer at once with a curious sense of security; and in September of 1926 I came to Northampton as to the haven where I would be. Nor have I since that day ever, for the fraction of a second, wanted to be elsewhere.

2

It is difficult at close range to write clearly and
fairly about a place and a person both of which
have fulfilled all one's expectations and desires.
Retrospection escapes in a measure such difficulties, for in looking back upon any experience at all
the mind is apt to seize upon and bring into sharp
relief only the things of value which have marked
that past experience. Yet my thirteen years in
Northampton possess a past as well as a present;
and since in retrospect my first year here has been
almost identical with my last in its offerings, I
must feel that memory and actuality, the past and
the present, for once unite to present an honest, if
an individual, point of view.

Northampton to those who know it is the most
pleasant of towns, and the valley in which it is
situated one of the most satisfactory of places. The
Holyoke and Tom ranges cut the sky with their
sharp outlines; the wide Connecticut flows slowly
below them. In the spring the orchards roundabout are white with blossoming fruit trees and
the pastures with laurel; in the autumn the flaming Berkshires bring the New Jerusalem from a
dream to a reality. For one to whom work on the
land is a never-failing source of pleasure the
onion and the tobacco fields of the Connecticut
valley are lavish in their gifts. The tiny, pale-green
spear-points of the onions pricking the brown soil

add resilience and buoyancy to the spring; and the Polish women who kneel on the soil between the rows give to these New England fields an added age and dignity by connecting them with longer years of labor in an older land. I have often wondered since I came to this valley to live whether art or necessity designed the long, symmetrical tobacco barns which stand at well-placed intervals upon the wide fields. Their outlines are so exactly right that they shame the ugly contours of certain of the farm-houses which exist because of them. The humid heat of summer, which here holds for weeks on end what Charles Lamb calls the dignity in extremes, brings out the heavy, pungent smell of both onions and tobacco so that a country walk makes one's nose tingle with the incense of the soil.

Like Lamb I have always felt the genius of places, that curious power which places possess of making one suddenly at home or not at home. The blue September haze over the fragrant valley on the day of my arrival within it, the early colors on the hills, the wide, clear river, birds gathering among the trees to go, and, last of all, a small red pail left by some child in the garden of the house where I was to live—these made me oddly sure that I had reached my home.

Northampton is a superior town in its own life quite apart from that of the college. Unlike many college towns it has an existence of its own which contributes to the life of the college quite as much as the college to it. Settled early, in 1634, by substantial Puritan families, it has retained its substantiality and many of its families. Its beautiful trees and pleasant streets, its fine old houses, its churches and schools, make it an enviable place of residence; and no member of the college faculty who sets up his household gods within it is unconscious of its offerings. Town and gown in Northampton know less separation than is common elsewhere under similar circumstances; and my friendships among Northampton people form one of my strongest reasons for continued residence within its borders.

Of Smith College it is difficult to write with calmness and circumspection since it has provided me, pressed down and running over, with life of the body, mind, and spirit for thirteen years. I cannot, indeed, imagine thirteen years more fully or beneficently spent under other possible circumstances. The feeling of confidence and respect with which I concluded my first year here has increased with the conclusion of twelve others; nor has any opportunity of teaching elsewhere during this span of time held the slightest temptation to me.

It is difficult to analyze satisfaction and contentment, to look for their sources. One is tempted to accept gratefully such a rare state of existence and let it go at that. Yet since this chapter is about Smith College rather than about myself, I shall attempt to put on paper for the first time the sources of my assurance that I would be nowhere else under the sun than in a small white house on a pleasant street fittingly known as Paradise Road, a part of the Smith College campus.

I like, first of all, the attitude of the college toward education in general, whether of men or of women. For Smith is not entrenched within any baseless notions that the minds and capacities of women are inferior to those of men and that they, therefore, require a different training. The position of the college toward education, its ideal, if you will, is the education of the entire personality of the student. It is concerned not alone with intellectual training, foremost and unlimited as that may be, but with character and aesthetic development, with health and the intelligent use of recreation, with social interests and obligations, with knowledge of contemporary affairs, with respect for tradition and for the wisdom both of the past and the present. Recognizing the fact that no two persons are alike, it is concerned with adapting itself to the individual so that each student may find herein the necessities and the nourishments for her own peculiar make-up. Its aim becomes, then, the enlightenment of communities through the enlightenment of its students, the raising of American life generation by generation to a higher standard of living through its thinking, its feeling, and its taste.

I do not for a moment mean to suggest that this

educational attitude of Smith is different from or superior to that of many other colleges. But I do feel, from a fairly wide acquaintance with others both directly and indirectly, that there is less talking about aims and, therefore, more accomplishing of them here than on many other campuses, largely, perhaps, because over-seriousness and introspection are not emphasized and because students are treated like intelligent human beings, capable for the most part of directing their own destinies.

From the start I liked the faculty at Smith, and I have increasingly liked it as recent years have brought to it the best possible people from this and other countries. The two hundred men and women who comprise our teaching staff are representative of many personalities and many points of view. Yet I do not believe there is anywhere a group of persons with greater tolerance, even respect, for the opinions of their colleagues. We represent all sorts of religious faiths, and none; all manner of political opinions, and none; all kinds of educational theories, and none. We are orthodox and heretic; conservative and liberal; practical and aesthetic; classical and romantic. We do not take ourselves too seriously, however, and for this very reason maintain in our association a kind of humorous balance which many college faculties lack. That enclosed pettiness, which certain suspicious and uninformed minds assume to be a quality peculiar to academic life, is surely not characteristic of the faculty at Smith. We live and let live; laugh and let laugh; fatten on the learning of our colleagues when we are lean ourselves; and for nine months of the year have about as good a time as is allotted to the race of men on earth

The brand of college student known as the Smith girl suits me admirably. I have seen girls come and go now for thirteen years, and, although I think that the past decade with its national and international catastrophes has improved the present output, I have been vastly satisfied with the lot as a whole. Most of our students come from homes of taste and background regardless of financial security, of which many possess much, more something, and some none at all. Most have been well trained in good schools; practically all are decently read; most are intelligent and eager.

I do not know greater pleasure than association and companionship with such students. This has been especially true in recent years when the loss of family fortunes and the curtailment of family incomes have brought about a new evaluation of intellectual and emotional wealth. The standard of college work, the interest in study both as a means to an end and as an end in itself, have immeasurably improved in the past years; and this very fact has immeasurably widened and deepened the friendships between teachers and students.

All college teachers of middle age, who can compare and contrast their present experience with their past, realize that at no other time has teaching been so pleasant and remunerative a profession, largely because of the associations which it affords outside the class-room even more than within it. The young today seem to recognize no barriers of age. People are people to them whatever their number of years, friendly or reserved, open-minded or closed, humorous or pedantic, likable or unattractive. They look upon their teachers much as they look upon their contemporaries and judge them by much the same standards. The result is a wholesomeness of relationship, a give and take of experiences and thoughts, which make teaching an exciting exchange of ideas rather than the imposition of them. The increased maturity in young people which this new age has effected has doubtless had its share in making this association with their elders more natural and pleasant. Perhaps it is this maturity that is responsible for the breaking down of barriers which a mere difference in age constructed during my own college days. But whatever has brought about this pleasant change of attitude of both teachers and students, the result has transformed teaching from a task into a companionship, which is at its best in Northampton and which is itself the third of the sources of my delight in Smith College.

3

It is to the president of Smith for the past twenty-two years that the college is forever indebted for its wholesome ideal of education, for the character and personality of its present faculty, and for the spirit of its students and its graduates; in other words, for itself. He came into a strong and noble tradition and he has increased its strength and its nobility. "To know how to suggest is the great art of teaching," writes Amiel in his *Journal;* and this knowledge has marked the administration of William Allan Neilson from the day when he came from Cambridge to Northampton in 1917 until he retired from the presidency of Smith last June. In this sense he has been a teacher far more than an administrator; or perhaps it would be more accurate to say that this art of suggestion, this power of the best of teaching, has marked every detail of his administration at Smith.

A great teacher himself, his first and foremost concern at Smith has been his faculty. We who have taught *with* him rather than *under* him, learned early those things which he expected of his colleagues. To be lukewarm in thinking and in teaching has been to him an insult to the profession. Better the most individual and fervid of opinions than no opinions at all; better the most unleashed of enthusiasms than the want of any predilections and passions. To be dishonest with one-

self or with one's students; to confuse values; to be
jealous of one's own advancement at the expense
of one's fellows; to harbor resentments or to be in-
dignant over fancied slights; to lack sympathy
openly with slow or with uncongenial minds; to
waste time in unprofitable pursuits; to see the particular rather than the universal; to lack respect
for past wisdom or to look with consternation
upon present ideas simply on the ground of their
newness; to fail in the understanding of human
emotions or to be insensible to human tragedy; to
be unable to laugh over matters which time will
prove inconsequential;—all these are attitudes of
mind which to him merit not so much scorn as
regret.

He has looked upon each member of his faculty
as an individual and has been anxious for the well-
being of the part in order to secure the well-being
of the whole. He has seen that teaching is made
more lively and productive when the teacher is
himself a student, a scholar of the best sort. To
this end he has been impatient with those of us
who find our teaching alone sufficient to exhaust
our days; and from the start of his presidency at
Smith he has sought to lighten teaching hours or
to arrange them in such a way that the teacher
shall have time and energy for his own research or
for articles and books of another character. I,
among many others, have cause to thank him for
days free of teaching that I might continue with

my writing. He has been the first to receive from us the outward and visible signs that we have not misused our leisure provided by him; and always we have known that any book or article published, any work in art or music or science accomplished, is in his mind not so much a distinction won for the college as a proof that, since we are not stagnating as individuals, our teaching is productive and alive.

To each and every member of his faculty he has been a friend and companion rather than a superior. His far-reaching, all-enfolding humanity has constantly brought to his office or to his home those in need of advice or of sympathy; and no one of us has ever been sent empty away. Ethical decisions, family difficulties, financial problems, love affairs, professional questions, broken hearts—all these have found entrance into his sometimes tired mind but always ready understanding. He probably harbors more secrets than most persons on this earth. Surely no one living has received more gratitude than he. A young instructor with a longing for new clothes and with no money to buy them; a father with a problem child; a man with a misfit as a wife; an unpopular and puzzled teacher; two persons at variance over something or other; those in emotional situations of any sort; those whom death or life, disaster or disappointment have darkened and who can find no light for themselves. For twenty-two years all such burdens have been dumped upon him by all of us, for we know that help has never been refused. And often there has been added to his own understanding that of a charming and lovely woman, whose companionship with her husband has been the ideal of many homes and whose quiet, humorous hold on life has given strength and reality to us all.

Mr. Neilson's way with his two thousand undergraduates has differed little from his way with his faculty. I think it is safe to say that no other college president has been so loved by his students. His personal charm is responsible in part for this devotion; his liking for them, in part also; his honesty, his knowledge of human nature, his humor, and his wisdom complete the reasons for his hold upon them. In too many colleges there is antagonism between the student body and the administration. In twenty-two years this has been unknown at Smith. Mr. Neilson has expected the co-operation of his students, and has received it. He has believed that what most students want is, or can be made, identical with what they ought to have, and his belief has been justified. He has welcomed suggestions and dissatisfactions from his undergraduates, and has dealt fairly with them and their desires. He has contended that to deal with common honesty and frankness with a student body is all that is needed to insure a friendly relationship; and his contention has never been disproved.

He has treated his undergraduates as persons

rather than as students. He has assumed their maturity and their power of wise decision, their ability to use time to good effect both at study and elsewhere; and his confidence has resulted in far fewer disappointments than in most colleges. As mature persons he has wanted them to live in a larger world than that bounded by the college gates; and his Monday morning chapel talks on world affairs have been invaluable toward this end. He has constantly tried to make them see that one's obligations to oneself and to others are better standards to live by than an insistence upon one's rights. He has had the genius to talk to them neither as one in authority nor as one of superior wisdom, but rather as a more experienced and understanding friend.

"The secret of people's getting on together," he once said to students and faculty alike, "is a secret of changing the emphasis from trying to grab for oneself the maximum to that of trying to find out how much one can give, how much one can do, how completely one can fulfill duty and obligation. This is in itself a very simple idea—full of difficulty, of course, when one tries to carry it out, because of one's appetites and desires, one's indignations and resentments. But whenever you find in any group of people a deadlock, a difficulty in getting common work done, you will find that it arises from the fact that each is concerned with his or her rights and not with his or her opportunities to serve. The moment the emphasis changes from rights to opportunities, the deadlock is broken, the clash removed, and the thing becomes perfectly simple."

He has never minced matters with his students. They have learned upon many occasions the objects of his contempt, even of his anger: dishonesty of any sort, from lying and cheating to an unrecognition or a subtle shifting of blame; laziness; vulgarity; the lack of personal responsibility; thoughtlessness of others. But his humor has always at once tempered and made more lasting in effect what the undergraduates term his "scoldings". I have never, in fact, heard him reprove his students without giving them the opportunity to laugh with him before he was through. When the question of smoking came up early in his administration and girls were misusing the privileges granted to them, he said in chapel:

"Smoking is a dirty, expensive, and unhygienic habit, to which I am devoted."

On one occasion when it was reported to him that two of his undergraduates had been swimming in the public reservoir with their friends from Yale, or Amherst, or some other of the nearby colleges which provide sufficient companionship, his anger in chapel was memorable. His last words, however, were more so.

"I want," he said, "to make you understand distinctly from this day forth that neither the citi-

zens of Northampton nor the members of the
college care to have their drinking water flavored
with Smith or Yale, Amherst, Harvard, or Williams."

He has wanted, perhaps above everything else,
that the college shall be a community of busy and
happy people, a place rich and pleasant in companionship. He and Mrs. Neilson have opened their
home upon numberless occasions to students, and
he has liked to know that the members of his faculty have done the same. I remember especially
something which he once said to me early in my
years at Smith. I had gone to his office to ask if
I might for one year be freed from Freshman
English. I asked this not because I disliked teaching freshmen or even reading their themes, but
because, as I told him, if one were even passably
decent to them, they were omnipresent with their
friendly invitations to tea or dinner. I had no time, I
said, for anything else if I acceded to their desires.

I remember the quizzical smile with which he
listened to my complaints. When I had finished,
he said:

"Now I could let you off from teaching, I suppose, or from reading your themes, but I really
couldn't let you off from tea and dinner. Perhaps
you don't know it yet, but to go to tea and dinner
with freshmen happens to be the most important
thing you're doing around this place. So run along
and do it. Remember that a teacher who isn't asked

to tea and dinner probably isn't worth her salt, and don't come asking again to be let off from what is your most important job to this college."

Thousands of women both young and middle-aged remember countless things which President Neilson has said to them. But among them all one stands pre-eminent: the urging upon them of cultivating within themselves by definite practice the ability and the desire to be frequently alone, in order that they may see their noisy days and years as but "moments in the being of the eternal Silence". Over and over again he has said these words or others like them:

"The person who can afford to be alone with himself often and long acquires a quality of personal dignity which is dissipated and lost in any other kind of life. . . . The self-possession, self-restraint, patience, which come only through the practice of solitude—these are essentials for the acquisition of a philosophy and a religion. And it makes all the difference in the world to your life whether you arrive at a philosophy and a religion or not. It makes the difference between living in a world which is merely a constantly changing mass of phenomena, and living in a significant, ordered universe."

4

As I read over what I have written about President Neilson, I discover that I have unconsciously avoided the past tense. This is as it should be. It is difficult to realize that when his college re-opens in September he will not be present to speak to teachers and students and to re-establish the pleasant, abundant order of our days together. Yet he is forever present in those realities which he has made abiding and secure in the minds of all those who have lived and worked with him.

Wisdom exalteth her sons and taketh hold of them that seek her. He that loveth her loveth life; and they that seek her early shall be filled with gladness. He that holdeth her fast shall inherit glory; and where he entereth, the Lord will bless. If he trust her, he shall inherit her; and his generations shall have her in possession.

And since, because of his generosity of time and encouragement, this book has been written, since he more than any other has suggested its name and established its faith in the goodly fellowship of those who teach and those who learn, it is fitting that he himself should conclude it with the conclusion of his last address to Smith College. For in this vision of another great scholar is seen his own, familiar to all who know him, the vision of those great and little things of the human spirit, the desire for which he has given to thousands, the possession of which is within himself:

"Twenty-one years ago I pledged myself in this place to uphold certain things for which the College had always stood, and I described them in the words of a great scholar. I cannot close today better than by quoting these words again. 'All these things are good,' he says, after enumerating the worthy desires of many men's hearts, 'All these things are good, and those who pursue them may well be soldiers in one army or pilgrims on the same eternal quest. If we fret and argue and fight one another now, it is mainly because we are so much under the power of the enemy. The enemy has no definite name, though in a certain degree we all know him: he who puts always the body before the spirit, the dead before the living; who makes things only to sell them; who has forgotten that there is such a thing as truth, and measures the world by advertisement or by money; who daily defiles the beauty that surrounds him and makes vulgar the tragedy; whose innermost religion is the worship of the lie in his soul. The Philistine, the vulgarian, the great sophist, the passer of base coin for true, he is all about us and, worse, he has his outposts inside us, persecuting our peace, spoiling our sight, confusing our values, making a man's self seem greater than the race and the present thing more important than the eternal. From him and his influence we find our escape by means of old books into that calm world of theirs where stridency and clamour are forgotten in the ancient stillness, where the strong iron is long since rusted, and the rocks of granite broken into dust, but the great things of the human spirit still shine like stars pointing man's way onward to the great triumph or the great tragedy; and even the little things, the beloved and tender and funny and familiar things, beckon across gulfs of death and change, with a magic poignancy, the old things that our dead leaders and forefathers loved, *viva adhuc et desiderio pulcriora,* living still and more beautiful because of our desire.' "